HOW TO UNDERSTAND THE BIBLE

A Practical Guide to Scriptural Clarity

Dr. Chika I. Egeruo

Independently published

Copyright © 2025 by Israel C. Egeruo.

All rights reserved. No part of this book may be used or reproduced in any form whatsoever without written permission except in the case of brief quotations in critical articles or reviews.

Unless otherwise noted, all scriptures are from the King James Version, public domain.

Scripture quotations marked NKJV are taken from the New King James Version®. Copyright © 1982 by Thomas Nelson. Used by permission. All rights reserved.

Scripture quotations marked NIV are taken from the Holy Bible, New International Version®, NIV®. Copyright © 1973, 1978, 1984, 2011 by Biblica, Inc.® Used by permission. All rights reserved worldwide.

Scripture quotations marked ESV are from the ESV® Bible (The Holy Bible, English Standard Version®), copyright © 2001 by Crossway, a publishing ministry of Good News Publishers. Used by permission. All rights reserved.

Printed in the United States of America.

For more information, contact:

Email: mydoveplace@gmail.com

Book design by the Author

Cover design by KC Anderson

ISBN - Paperback: 978-2-7255-0791-0

First Edition: April 2025

PREFACE

This book aims to demonstrate how to read and understand the Bible, an exploration designed to help you unveil its hidden treasures. At first glance, the title might seem elusive, a deliberate choice to welcome all perspectives without raising objections. Yet, behind this veil lies a passionate quest to provide a compass for navigating the pages of Scripture and discerning its profound truths.

The intention to write a spiritual book of this magnitude was born out of an insuppressible urge that stems from its necessity in an era where truth appears to wane and spiritual waters are clouded by transactional and motivational religiosity. It is, therefore, crucial to address issues that will set the path straight for earnest truth-seekers, equipping them with the ability to discern, filter, and embrace pure, untainted, and unadulterated truth.

To achieve this, the book promotes a culture of individual Bible study among devoted believers passionate about the Lord. This habit has become increasingly rare among modern-day Christians. Surprisingly, many blame their lack of Bible reading on its perceived difficulty, while others claim that the apparent contradictions within Scripture discourage them. Still, many rely solely on their preachers' sermons, creating a community of believers who remain spiritual infants, lacking the revelational knowledge of God's Word.

But behold, dear reader! Within these pages lies the transformative solution: the art of engaging with the Bible, unraveling its wisdom through diligent study and better comprehension.

This book is written for those engaged in authentic worship, seekers of personal spiritual growth, those misled by alternative teachings, and anyone facing deception due to a limited understanding of Scripture. Suppose you have ever struggled to interpret the Bible accurately or found yourself caught in misconceptions passed down by others. In that case, this book offers you a lifeline—a chance to master the skills to uncover and embrace biblical truth as it was meant to be understood.

Every believer must prioritize accurate scriptural understanding because each misinterpretation leads to misguided practices, faulty decisions, and a disconnect from the author's original intent. Moreover, distorted biblical teachings pose a grave challenge to Christianity, leading to misrepresentation, misleading doctrines, and the emergence of a pseudo-Christianity shaped by misunderstood scriptures. The Master Himself placed great importance on knowing the truth, declaring:

"*If ye continue in my word, then are ye my disciples indeed. And ye shall know the truth, and the truth shall make you free.*"

This statement also emphasizes the necessity of personal and continual engagement with Scripture, as genuine discipleship hinges on sound biblical comprehension—a path toward embodying true Christianity.

To fully benefit from the skills taught in this book, readers must ensure that everything they believe about God, His interactions, and His revelations aligns with Scripture. This principle is crucial yet often overlooked in today's Christian community, where many accept teachings without scrutiny. The reason for this insistence is simple: The Bible is the ultimate authority in Christianity, just as a nation's constitution governs its citizens. When someone acts against the law of the land, they face consequences because they have strayed from the nation's guiding principles. Likewise, straying from biblical truth means straying from God's intended path. The bottom line is clear: If the Bible doesn't say it, God didn't authorize it—meaning it is not His word.

This book will serve as a clear and practical guide to help you navigate the Bible properly and confidently. You'll learn the essential steps to take when reading or studying Scripture, ensuring you grasp its intended messages rather than misinterpret them.

A practical guide to scriptural clarity

We'll explore the fundamental principles of biblical interpretation, shedding light on overlooked yet crucial insights that the Bible provides for those seeking to understand its message. Additionally, we'll examine common pitfalls many fall into when they fail to apply these principles—and why avoiding them is so important.

Each step will be illustrated with real-world examples and supported by scriptural references, reinforcing the key concepts discussed. While you may notice some repetition throughout the book, this is intentional to drive home these truths and ensure they resonate deeply with you.

By the end, you'll have a stronger foundation for interpreting the Bible accurately and applying its wisdom to your life.

Read and let the Word of God speak to you.

Content

Preface V

1 The Book 1

2 Choosing The Right Version 12

3 Study 29

4 Literal Or Figurative 43

5 Rules Of Bible Interpretation 51

6 Add Not, Subtract Not 71

7 Rightly Divide 79

8 Guidance Of The Spirit 110

9 Starting Your Biblical Journey 116

10 Pitfalls To Avoid 131

11 A Practical Guide 141

12 Final Words 151

Index 155

1

THE BOOK

The Bible is God's continual communication with humanity. However, there has been a continuous debate between the Bible being God's word and men's work. Additionally, an alternative view is emerging that openly rejects the notion that the Bible is entirely God's word or the product of human authors. This new thought opined that the Bible contains the word of God, but not entirely God's word, since several characters spoke in it, including the devil. What does the Bible reveal regarding its origins, author, and voice without further getting into these arguments? Well, to answer that question, we must choose the Bible's own words in 2nd Timothy chapter 3 verse 16:

All scripture is given by inspiration of God…

By inspiration, the scripture implies that God empowered humans to write using human language, conveying words with the same essence and meaning as His own. To grasp the depth of what it means for a text to be "inspired by God," let's explore it with a relatable example. Imagine a professional who relies on a scribe, perhaps a personal assistant or secretary, to record their conversations with clients, draft correspondence, or prepare speeches for public presentations. The scribe meticulously documents these exchanges, always attributing the content to the employer. When someone later reads these documents, they naturally perceive them as the employer's words, even though the scribe physically wrote them down. The essence, intent, and authority behind the words belong entirely to the employer.

In the same way, inspiration works; it is God's voice and message conveyed through the hands of those who document it. The account still reflects the employer's perspective when the scribe records a narrative in which the employer recounts someone else's words. It would still be considered the employer's side of the story even if the presentation features exact quotes from a third party. This explains how each of these human writers who played the role of God's scribes, as illustrated above, was specially and divinely inspired and directed to write. For example, the author of the book of Jeremiah described how the LORD, God of Israel, gave him the command to "write in a book all the words He has spoken to him" (Jeremiah 30:2). This is a straightforward instruction to document the word coming from the Lord. This story is comparable to the author of the book of Habakkuk's testimony, which reads;

And the LORD answered me, and said, Write the vision, and make it plain upon tables, that he may run that readeth it (Habakkuk 2:2).

Similarly, several prophets claimed to have written the words of the Lord, including Isaiah (1:2), Ezekiel (1:3), Jonah (1:1), and Micah (1:1). Even though numerous other authors with whom God communicated may not have shared the stories of their inspiration, it is straightforward to understand and accept that they were equally involved in the divine process as God's scribes just like others who shared theirs, and the process led to the writing of the scriptures. Although we have read over and over that the prophets received words and instructions from the Lord God, it is important to note that God empowered them through His holy Spirit (2 Peter 1:21). All our discussions in this book, therefore, will assume the reader believes that God inspired all the scripture. Acknowledging the Bible as being breathed by God seems to be a fair ground to establish the skills required to understand the Bible. This does not rule out the understanding that many bible readers do not believe in the existence of God. The benefits such unbelieving readers seek from the Bible may not be found within the scope of this written piece.

This chapter is meant to introduce the Bible as a book. Therefore, the question is, what kind of book is the Bible? How different people or groups read and use the Bible may give them different answers to this question. But the truth is that the Bible is God's note to his children. We can also say that there are many parts to the Bible. It is the basis for Christians' faith and practice, a record of history, a literary masterpiece, a source of moral and ethical advice, a theological treatise, an instruction manual, and a canonical collection of different writings. The book's depth and breadth have made it one of the most important in history.

The Bible provides numerous benefits that are centered on making the reader conform to the image of Christ. This simply means that reading, understanding, and acting on the words in the Bible transform the individual into the likeness of Christ, a perfect man. 2 Timothy 3:16-17 puts it in simple terms:

All scripture is given by inspiration of God, and is profitable for doctrine, for reproof, for correction, for instruction in righteousness: That the man of God may be perfect, thoroughly furnished unto all good works.

The Christian Bible comprises numerous books, but there's no consensus on the exact count. Among Protestants, 66 books are commonly accepted as the canon, while the Ethiopian Orthodox Church acknowledges 81. Other Christian denominations vary in acceptance, falling somewhere between these two ranges. For this book, we will limit our discussion to the generally accepted 66 books of the Bible, which include Genesis, Exodus, Leviticus, Numbers, Deuteronomy, Joshua, Judges, Ruth, 1 Samuel, 2 Samuel, 1 Kings, 2 Kings, 1 Chronicles, 2 Chronicles, Ezra, Nehemiah, Esther, Job, Psalms, Proverbs, Ecclesiastes, Song of Solomon, Isaiah, Jeremiah, Lamentations, Ezekiel, Daniel, Hosea, Joel, Amos, Obadiah, Jonah, Micah, Nahum, Habakkuk, Zephaniah, Haggai, Zechariah, Malachi in the Old Testament, and Matthew, Mark, Luke, John, Acts, Romans, 1 Corinthians, 2 Corinthians, Galatians, Ephesians, Philippians, Colossians, 1 Thessalonians, 2 Thessalonians, 1 Timothy, 2 Timothy, Titus, Philemon, Hebrews, James, 1 Peter, 2 Peter, 1 John, 2 John, 3 John, Jude Revelation in the New Testament.

These 66 books were written over 1,500 years by 40 distinct authors but have one consistent storyline running all the way through, which centers on God's plan, conceived in eternity, made known via the prophets, and executed by God the Son, Jesus Christ, to save humans from the terrible effects of the Fall.

Scholars and biblical evidence suggest that Moses authored the first five books of the Old Testament, collectively known as the Pentateuch, beginning around 1450 BC. Remarkably, many of the events recorded by Moses occurred centuries before his time. This knowledge was revealed to him by God, enabling him to document significant historical and divine events, such as the creation of the world and humanity, which he could not have personally witnessed. Moses himself affirmed that he wrote down the words of the Lord, as noted in Exodus 24:4.

As confirmed by archaeological discoveries, writing was already a well-developed practice during Moses' lifetime. Various materials were used for writing, including stone inscriptions, clay tablets with cuneiform script, animal hides, and wooden surfaces. It is widely believed that Moses wrote in Hebrew, the language of the Israelites, and likely recorded his writings on animal hides in a scroll-like format.

As Israel's history unfolded, additional books were added to the Hebrew Scriptures beyond Moses' contributions. The compilation of the Hebrew canon continued until approximately 420 BC, concluding with the book of Malachi.

The New Testament, which appeared to be a continuation from Malachi in the Christian Bible or the start of a new dispensation in a proper view, came to us years after Jesus had ascended. During His earth walk, Jesus read and cited the Old Testament of the Christian bible, which was then available, and spent years teaching His disciples, imparting knowledge that would later form part of the New Testament. He unveiled His identity to humanity through the Scriptures. He taught that all scriptures were about Him, drawing on the writings of Moses and other Old Testament prophets (Luke 24:27). It is of the utmost importance to emphasize that Jesus' teachings were inspired by the same source that gave origin to the Old Covenant, God. This is why Jesus said, *for I have not spoken of myself; but the Father which sent me, he gave me a commandment, what I should say, and what I should speak* (John 12:49).

Just before His crucifixion, Jesus promised His disciples that the Holy Spirit, sent by the Father in His name, would teach them all they needed to know and act as a continual reminder of His teachings (John 14:26). This promise was fulfilled starting on the day of Pentecost. So, all the disciples who were involved in writing the books contained in the New Testament first received the Holy Spirit. This implies that, similar to the Old Testament, the Holy Spirit guided and inspired different human instruments to write the New Testament. For example, the apostle Paul, who is credited with writing most of the New Testament books, stated, *For I have received of the Lord that which also I delivered unto you…* (1 Corinthians 11:23).

Take note of the word "Lord," which appears in his testimony and frequently in the stories of the Old Covenant prophets, as the source of their information. In a similar vein, John, the author of the book of Revelation, explained how God also gave him the words he wrote:

A practical guide to scriptural clarity

And he that sat upon the throne said, Behold, I make all things new. And he said unto me, Write: for these words are true and faithful (Revelation 21:5).

The apostles acknowledge that the Holy Spirit moved the individuals involved in writing the entire Bible, which is why Peter stated in 2 Peter 1:21, *for prophecy never came by the will of man, but [a]holy men of God spoke as they were moved by the Holy Spirit* (NKJV). Thus, we can confidently affirm that although human hands put together the writings in Matthew through Revelation, God Himself inspired them. Therefore, we may also say that the content of these books is the exact message that God wants to be preserved for the entire world.

The Jewish people were involved in developing the Old Testament, and most of its writings originated in Israel. The writings of Daniel, Ezekiel, and Esther, written during the Babylonian captivity, were outliers. Many New Testament books were written in different parts of the Roman Empire, with Luke's Gospel and Acts being the only two not written by Jews. For example, Paul wrote his epistles from multiple locations, including Rome and Corinth. Furthermore, the New Testament writings spread gradually due to the slow process of duplicating texts by hand. Some books were written within two decades of these events, while most were finished before the second century.

Concerning the authorship of the books of the New Testament, insisting on digging for the authors of each of the books may not benefit much. Since we are certain of the content's legitimacy, it would be preferable to realize that the writers have less influence over the writing than the substance itself. On the other hand, if a script is written after a disciple's name, there's no reason to question their authorship. When a Bible book is referred to as John, for instance, it implies that John was the author. That explains why it is generally accepted that this disciple either wrote the work named after them themselves, upon being inspired to do so, or enlisted the help of a third person.

Several books have been written on how we got the Bible, with diverse suggestions. But it's also critical to be mindful that, despite their seeming age, reading materials authored by circular scholars may be problematic when determining where we obtained our Bible. Such writers' prejudices might obscure some truths that could emerge from these investigations. The above may account for the debates over the history of the Bible's trajectory. The Bible, interestingly, hints at its source and should suffice since our belief in God and Christ is not in any way found on the pages of history books but on faith alone.

Finally, regarding the books in our canon, one might wonder what evidence supports the selection of the 66 books that make up the Bible. How can we be certain that these specific books are the right ones, neither more nor less than what should be included in our Holy Book? A thorough answer to this question would necessitate a long doctrinal essay. But, in summary, the Old Testament established a canon of its own, having already been put together as the Jewish Torah. In contrast, the New Testament books need to pass the test of scriptural inclusivity to be acknowledged.

The test of scriptural inclusivity, so worded, comprises five questions: Is it the work of an apostle? Does it sound plausible enough? Has it been in use from the beginning of time? Are most churches making use of it? Does it follow the church's orthodox teachings? These assessments identified the books that met the scriptural criteria and were thus eligible for canonization. There could not have been errors in this process since God, the author, has affirmed to preserve his words, just as the Psalmist sang:

Forever, O Lord, thy word is settled in heaven" (Psalm 119:89).

As a summary of this chapter, we have seen that all scripture, whether Old Testament or New Testament, was inspired by God. Holy men of God were moved to document what we have today as the Bible. God set these men apart (Holy) to accomplish this task. Historians narrated that the scribes who produced copies of the scripture followed stringent procedures during the exercise: washed hands before and after writing, dedicated special pens, one especially for writing the name of God, and washed hands before and after writing the name of God, and exact words proceeding from the mouth of God. That depicts the level of seriousness we should accord the words we read out of the Bible because they are God speaking to us.

2

CHOOSING THE RIGHT VERSION

The Bible version we read determines how we understand it and whether we are getting what God intended from the reading. We have established earlier that the Bible is inspired; from Matthew 5:18, we can also infer that every word, phrase, line, or idea was inspired; in other words, they came from God. Since every word in the Bible came from God, it would be wrong for any man to change or alter a single word. God could have picked the words that would change the written ones, but He would rather have chosen the ones he chose, and we should not find ourselves trying to correct or help Him. This should be simple to agree with, but suppose you still doubt this assertion and argue that just because a word is inspired doesn't mean it can't be changed, or for those who think that the idea that a single letter or word can't be changed might be overly restrictive of a rule. Hear what the Bible says in Matthew 5:18 to that effect:

For verily I say unto you, Till heaven and earth pass, one jot or one tittle shall in no wise pass from the law, till all be fulfilled.

From the above Bible verse, we can conclude that every word counts and is equally important. These words are fixed in heaven and are even more stably fixed than the whole creation of God. However, when we say the words are inspired, we must remember that the original inspired text was never in English. So, the English Bible, as we have it in our hands today, is a product of several processes, including translations and laborious copying of the original scripts of the various books that comprise the Bible.

Regarding the translation process that results in the various Bible Versions available today, we know that the Old and New Testaments were first written in Aramaic and Greek, respectively, then translated into many other languages, including our dear English from both sides. Today, the Bible is available in approximately fifty English-language translations or versions. Interestingly, these English translations do not carry identical wording in every verse, hinting that the content may differ. Does that imply that the scripts' processes may have introduced subtle alterations in the word of God? It seems so; the discrepancy in these Bible versions seems to indicate certain modifications. If not, why would different translations from the same source portray different words or ideas? It makes sense to say that some Bible versions would have altered the words of God, even though doing so is discouraged. The point we want to establish here is that not all Bible versions on the shelf today carry the message God intends to pass to humanity, since these versions have changed what God gave the original writers to document in the scriptures. There is a lot of proof of such modifications in many of the more recent Bible versions. For example, in certain portions, the King James version of the bible (both old and new versions) contains some important phrases omitted in several other translations.

Look at 1 John 5:7, for instance, we see an important statement that reads.

For there are three that bear witness in heaven: the Father, the Word, and the Holy Spirit; and these three are one (NKJV).

This key statement, also seen in the King James Version (KJV), was completely omitted in certain bible translations, notably in the two most recent versions of the Bible, the English Standard Version (ESV) and the New International Version (NIV). A similar omission is observed in Matthew 17:21, which is read in KJV as *Howbeit this kind goeth not out but by prayer and fasting.* A statement, both the New King James Version (NKJV) and the KJV also carried, but was omitted in both the NIV and ESV. These omissions are not peculiar to the above Bible versions; they abound from one translation to another, not just in the versions mentioned. But the question one needs to ask is, are these omissions significant? Well, yes, they are, and we may have seen the reason earlier when we observed that these words are settled in heaven and, therefore, need not be tampered with.

Even the slightest changes to the Bible's words can significantly impact our faith, as they risk altering the message God intended to communicate to His children. Each modification can lead to shifts in understanding, belief, and practice. Nonetheless, the above and several other omissions are discovered in these most recent translations of the bible, such as the ones found in John 5:4, Acts 8:37, and others.

It might also interest you to know that these omissions are not mere mistakes. The argument backing these deliberate omissions found in these modern Bible translations is that the phrases are also absent in the critical texts, the manuscripts from which these versions are translated. According to the argument, since the translation of the King James Version in 1611, numerous manuscripts have emerged. A wealth of additional studies has been accessible. Most of the newly discovered manuscripts lacked those extra phrases in the manuscript from which the King James Version was translated. These newly discovered manuscripts were also believed to be relatively older than the KJV's manuscript. Therefore, certain sections are either not included in newer versions or accompanied by footnotes that further explain the manuscript's content.

Simply put, the translators of the newer versions believe that the initial versions they discovered do not have the words or phrases they omitted in their newer versions of the Bible. Two interesting questions are: first, is there any evidence that the older the manuscript, the better it is? Secondly, why were these manuscripts unavailable when the KJV was translated, or why were they ignored? Suppose they were purposefully ignored, are we more knowledgeable, and closer to the truth than these ancient saints, to whom these bible accounts are fresher than it is to us? I do not think so!

The older manuscripts dug out and used by these modern translations are possibly erroneous copies of the original manuscript, left to naturally decay. Note that during the writing and copying of the original scripts, erroneous copies that were to be ridded of or destroyed were not because the scribes feared meddling with God's word, so they buried most of these scripts. It appears that the scripts seen as the older ones discovered may or may not be of these supposed-to-be destroyed pages because of the omissions they discovered at the time; after being discovered and termed older scripts, these, with omission, later found their way into these recent translations. We may not say this with resounding authority, but from history, we read that archeological digs have uncovered all these papyrus fragments. It is, therefore, safe to make the above assumptions.

There has been ongoing debate among scholars and believers regarding the discrepancies between various Bible versions. Some argue that the more recent versions are the most accurate since they are based on older manuscripts discovered after the compilation of the Textus Receptus, which is the widely accepted manuscript used since 1611. Others believe that these differences, though present, are minor and do not significantly alter the message. However, some firmly uphold the infallibility of the Textus Receptus. Among these groups is the "King James Only" movement, which asserts that the King James Version (KJV) is the only translation that fully preserves the infallible Word of God. Others acknowledge the KJV as the most reliable English translation but do not condemn those who use other versions. While I do not wish to engage in these debates, I place great trust in the King James Version and wholeheartedly recommend it to any believer seeking to study and understand the mind of God.

Moving away from the manuscript debates, there are other issues of concern around many of these newer translations, such as the unintentional deviation from the intended contextual meanings. Many of these differences found in several portions are thought to have been brought about by the translation procedure used in the most recent versions. Whereas most other translations are based on phrase-for-phrase translation, the KJV was translated word-for-word, which appears not to introduce any other person's notion but rather the exact exchange of words from one language to another. Worryingly, phrase-for-phrase translation, also known as idea-for-idea translation, depends largely on the interpreter's grasp of the phrase, which isn't great for maintaining the author's original meaning. This means that every translation using the phrase-for-phrase method becomes incorrect when the interpreter does not comprehend the translated phrase, idiom, or expression. Translating word-for-word emerged as a preferred choice because it minimizes the risk of inaccuracies in rendering the translated words. Other than the KJV, popular bible versions such as the New King James Version (NKJV), New American Standard Bible (NASB), and English Standard Version (ESV) enjoyed the word-for-word translation method. On the other hand, the New International Version (NIV) and the New Living Translation (NLT) are popular versions translated via the phrase-for-phrase method.

The word-for-word translation, formal equivalency, aims to keep as much of the original text's words and structure as possible. It lets readers interact with the content in a way that is like the original language's style and structure, keeping the original language's style and linguistic nuances. Word-for-word translating allows the translator to convey the idea of verbal inspiration and show that God intentionally picked each word in the original text. The goal is to maintain the inspired essence of the original words, representing them accurately and precisely while recognizing their sacred nature. This approach aligns with theological perspectives that emphasize the divine inspiration of the words in the Bible.

Formal equivalency closely follows the literal meaning of words and phrases, reducing the translator's subjective interpretation. Focusing on linguistic equivalence reduces the chance of unintentional biases or personal opinions influencing the translation. All these benefits are reflected in the KJV.

Formal equivalence is certainly not free of challenges. For example, to maintain a precise translation of the source material, formal equivalence frequently leads to sentences that sound awkward or unnatural in the target language. This can make it difficult for readers to understand the translated content, especially if the linguistic structures of the source and destination languages differ significantly. Formal equivalency keeps the literal meaning of idioms, expressions, and figures of speech from the source language. But this can also mean that the translated words don't always match how people talk in the target language, which can be confusing or unclear to people who don't know the details of the original language. Strict adherence to formal equivalency could lead to translations that demand more interpretation from readers. Readers may need to figure out the intended meaning because the focus is on preserving the original text's structure and vocabulary. This is especially true when dealing with language distinctive to a given situation or cultural references that could be difficult to translate. These are some common complaints from KJV readers, often ascribed to its difficulty and the archaic and Shakespearean English utilized in its writing.

However, the King James Version of the Bible was first published in 1611 and has been widely used for generations before the introduction of the Revised Version (RV) in 1881 and the American Standard Version (ASV) in 1901. Between the publication of the KJV and the next version, the RV is centuries apart, and Christianity did not halt during the intervening centuries. Christians continued their efforts to evangelize, win souls, and nurture new believers, relying on the King James version of the Bible. Congregations utilized the Bible, the KJV, in their fellowship. Therefore, there seems to be no pressing need for other versions of the Bible.

Nevertheless, it has been contended that the primary objective of the Revised Version was to offer a more precise and modernized translation of the Bible, which would resolve perceived deficiencies and incorporate the latest developments in biblical scholarship and linguistics. But the question many have asked is, was the revision necessary since the mandate of making disciples of all nations has remained effective with the King James version? It is also believed that the development of the RV was a British initiative that the Church of England initiated. A project that involved a collaborative effort of a committee of scholars from various denominations, who were motivated to improve the clarity and fidelity of the English translation in light of the advancements in understanding ancient manuscripts and languages since the publication of the King James Version. They sought to bring the English Bible closer to contemporary linguistic usage and scholarly knowledge. Despite how good this intention may sound, the idea of enhancement and modernity is not as harmless as it may seem. They subtly infuse human touches into the word and distort the author's original intent. This raises serious questions about the reliability of such translations, as some argue that most versions serve as vehicles for disseminating theological and denominational errors disguised as the Bible.

The widely perceived political correctness exhibited by some of the most recent bible versions is an obvious example of subtle human influences in the text. The latest edition of the New International Version (NIV), like many other modern translations, intentionally avoids using "he" or "him" as the default reference for an unspecified person but uses "they" instead. In Mark 1:17 of the NIV Bible, the phrase "'Come, follow me,' Jesus said, 'and I will send you out to fish for people'" replaces the traditional term "men" with "people." Similarly, the old translation of John's statement, "If anyone says, 'I love God,' yet hates his brother," has been updated to "brother or sister" in the new, politically correct translations.

In certain instances, the text also substitutes "whoever" for "he." These altered pronouns pose a threat because they may undermine the position of the scripture in the current ongoing debates on sexuality. Apart from the observed political correctness, many people argue that the NIV, the ESV, as well as some other translations, downplay the deity of Jesus Christ. For example, consider how ESV renders Philippians 2:6: "Who, though he was in the form of God, did not count equality with God a thing to be grasped," whereas in the KJV, it reads, *"who, being in the form of God, thought it not robbery to be equal with God."* The translations are at variance, the latter assures the deity of Jesus, the subject of the conversation, while the former seems not to loud it.

Many Pentecostal and evangelical churches today prefer modern Bible translations for their readability, but that shouldn't justify accepting their inaccuracies. After all, the Bible is meant to be studied, and true study requires effort. If we take the time to engage with the versions that shaped the faith for centuries before these newer translations appeared, we can still grasp the same life-changing messages that have saved and nurtured believers for generations.

On the side of the readability of the Bible, there is the New King James Version (NKJV), which is an entirely different translation of its own. Although the NKJV is a translation of its own, as already stated, it was mainly based on the KJV, which makes it not deviate as much from the KJV. The NKJV is made readable but maintains the literature style and tone of the KJV and is believed to be an update on the early English of the KJV. The major difference readily noticed in the NKJV is the change of certain archaic words such as 'thy' to 'your,' 'eth' to 's,' as seen in taketh to takes, giveth to gives, etc., and the use of the word 'Holy Spirit,' instead of Holy 'Ghost' to that effect.

That does not mean the New King James Version has no issues. Beyond the easily recognizable changes mentioned, there are issues that many of the lovers of the KJV frown at, such as certain obvious deviations from the KJV. For example, in Gen 22:8, the NKJV states, "God will provide for himself the lamb," while it reads, "*God will provide himself a lamb*" in the KJV. In Matt 18:26, the NKJV reads "before him saying, Master," but the KJV reads "*and worshipped him, saying, Lord*," and in Acts 3:13, 26, the NKJV reads "His Servant Jesus, " In contrast, the KJV reads "his Son Jesus." The NKJV seems to demote Jesus Christ in all these passages, as alleged in several other newer versions. The issue of modernization and political correctness also surfaced again in the NKJV; for example, in Genesis 2:18, "help meet for him"(KJV) was altered to "helper comparable to him."(NKJV), a translation that some have noted as favoring women's liberation, as it appears to dilute the distinction of the roles God designed for husbands and wives.

You might be getting worried and questioning why the discouragement. Well, if you must choose a bible version to read and understand the intent of God, the author, that choice must come from a place of knowledge and conviction. The information provided thus far is intended to guide your decision. As readers, it may seem practical to consult various versions of the Bible, turning to those with simpler language when others prove challenging. However, one must be mindful that an easily understood translation may, in some cases, reflect the translator's interpretation rather than the true intent of the original text. This underscores the importance of having a trusted version to read and familiarize oneself with its styles and mode of communication, irrespective of how difficult or easy it may initially appear.

If you have read this chapter thus far, you have likely discerned the Bible version I rely on. I wholeheartedly recommend the King James Version, as I believe it faithfully conveys the mind of God. We have given several reasons for this choice, including its foundation on the Textus Receptus, its nature as a word-for-word translation, and its remarkable endurance through the ages. Over time, it has nurtured both great and humble believers alike, including those who contributed to translating more recent Bible versions.

That does not mean we do not find one or two issues we worry about in the KJV; even some King James-only Crusaders find certain linguistic issues that are not fundamental and do not interfere with the message. A good example is the term holy ghost used several times in the New Testament. The King James Version of the Bible is the current English translation that uses that term. The Holy Ghost appears 90 times, whereas the most appropriate term, the 'Holy Spirit,' is mentioned 7 times in the King James Version. The rationale behind the KJV translators' decision to use "Ghost" in most instances and "Spirit" in a few remains unclear. I have gathered that in Shakespeare's and King James's day, the word "ghost" meant a person's vital spirit. The term "spirit" was originally used to describe the afterlife or a supernatural specter in that era. Moreover, the KJV translates identical Greek and Hebrew words as "ghost" and "spirit" in several instances, which helps to understand that the KJV translators did not want to convey the concept of "the spirit of a deceased person" when they used the term "ghost." But, as the language developed, the term "ghost" changed over time and came to mean the appearance of a person who had passed away, whereas "spirit" meant the very essence of life or any living thing. The fact that in our day, the spirit of a deceased person is depicted as a ghost makes it the wrong terminology for many believers.

A practical guide to scriptural clarity

Other linguistic issues include the use of numerous archaic words, which most are not used in our present day, such as agone, beseech, comely, dearth, extol, Goodspeed, and so many others, and lots of archaic verbs, sayest, taketh, and others. These may concern modern readers since these words are not our everyday words. Of course, these linguistic issues do not disqualify the KJV from flawlessness because they are not as fundamental as an incorrect translation of a message, the insertion of unintended material, or an omission from the Bible.

What we have seen over the years is that with constant use, these unfamiliar words become clearer over time, especially when the reader gets familiar with the KJV's poetic style. Also, we live in the digital age, when the internet's vast resources are readily available, allowing us to uncover answers and explore information with unprecedented ease.

On the other hand, I recently ran into a preacher who believes using these non-recent words in the KJV is helpful and strategic in understanding the Bible. The preacher contends that these words can bring clarity and specificity when studied. For example, in John Chapter 3, Jesus' usage of thee then Ye distinguishes between talking about Nicodemus singularly and mankind in the plural. More specifically, look at verse 7: *Marvel not that I said unto thee* (Nicodemus), *Ye* (everyone) *must be born again* (KJV). Thee in the sentence is singular, and Ye plural; thee alluded to Nicodemus, to whom he spoke, and Ye referred to all of humanity. It would be confusing if Jesus used 'you' in that line to refer to both Nicodemus and the entire world, which would be grammatically acceptable in recent English but could leave some readers with the perception that Jesus was simply stating that Nicodemus alone needed to be born again.

Notwithstanding, if the readability of the KJV presents a challenge for you and you feel compelled to use a more modern translation, it would be wise to keep a KJV alongside it for comparison, ensuring clarity and accuracy in your understanding. This ensures that the core message remains unchanged. For example, if you attend or lead a congregation that prefers any readable recent Bible versions to accommodate members of all literacy levels. Comparing all readings with a parallel KJV ensures that you stay aligned with its core message, whether delivering it to a congregation or reflecting on it personally.

You might be wondering if I endorse any other readable versions. However, my role is not to approve or dismiss any Bible versions. My recommendations are merely made from personal convictions and cannot replace the holy spirit in you, whom the master has promised will guide us into all truths. As a personal recommendation, I stand by the KJV. However, if the language poses a serious challenge, the New King James

Version (NKJV) is a good alternative. While it is a new translation, it stays largely faithful to the KJV.

As a final comment on the chapter, one may wonder why the author or some preachers who largely rely on the King James version of the Bible believe or make it a big deal. It is a big deal because most of these alternative bible translations stem from humans' desire to support their worldview. Most of these translators desired a bible that easily aligned with their message. For example, a congregation that does not believe in Christ's deity would choose a Bible version that downplays Christ's status as a member of the Godhead. That becomes misleading for a serious believer who reads it without preconceived notions. I sincerely desire that you choose a bible that will not deceive you but reveal God's intent to you.

3

STUDY

God's key purpose behind providing us with the Bible is to ensure we read and acquire His message. It is important to commence this chapter by emphasizing this once more. Look at the question Jesus asked in Luke 10:26: *He said unto him, What is written in the law? how readest thou?* Pay close attention to the last phrase, "*How readest thou?*" or more clearly, how do you read it? We can draw two vital inferences from this question. Firstly, it indicates that the scripture is meant to be read. Secondly, it emphasizes the significance of how it is read, which we shall spend some time on later. For context's sake, be mindful that the term "the law" in that sentence could specifically refer to certain portions or the entirety of the Old Testament. We are saying that Jesus asked the question because he knows the scripture is meant to be read. Similarly, when He was asked a question in the temple, He responded by asking, "Have ye never read?" (Matthew 21:16). Implying again that the scripture is to be read. That is why, in Acts 17:11, a congregation of dedicated believers who engaged in regular scripture reading was praised for doing so.

A practical guide to scriptural clarity

We cannot overemphasize the need to read the Bible, which is the intention behind God making it available to us, as already established. It is vital to consciously state this since this book has numerous misunderstandings. That is why many groups use it differently in the way they choose; for example, the court uses the Bible to swear. Some individuals view the Bible as a compendium of incantations, utilizing its contents to cast spells. Others regard it as an enigmatic tome shrouded in mystery. The largest faction perceives it as a sacred object for prayer, treating it as a symbolic representation of divine power. Another group considers it a protective talisman, keeping it beneath their pillows during sleep to ward off malevolent spirits or nightmares, or placing it behind the windshield of their vehicles to avert accidents. Unfortunately, those are incorrect uses of the Bible. The Bible is intended to be read and understood, and of course, in Matthew 24:15, the bible states; *whoso readeth, let him understand.* Emphasizing again that it must be read, and in addition, we must understand its content when we read it.

As previously mentioned, when Jesus asked, "How do you read it?" He may have been referring to the understanding of the text. However, we can also infer that the question highlighted the importance of how we approach or read the Scripture. This implies that our method of reading directly influences our understanding of it. How, then, should we engage with Scripture? To answer this, it is crucial to clarify that the more accurate term is "study" rather than simply "read," even though we have often used the latter. In other words, the Bible is meant to be studied. We frequently use the word "read" when discussing our engagement with books, including the Bible, yet simply reading the Bible will not provide the reader with the in-depth understanding they seek. Reading and studying have similarities but are distinct activities. Reading is the visual interpretation of written or printed text to understand its meaning or collect information, which can range from leisurely novel reading to acquiring facts from newspapers or websites.

On the other hand, studying is a more deliberate and active process that involves engaging with academic information to gain better knowledge, master a subject, or prepare for exams. Several tactics, such as note-taking, summarizing, and problem-solving, are used to internalize and retain information efficiently. While reading might be more passive and adaptable, studying necessitates concentrated effort and concentration, typically with learning objectives in mind.

One vital gain in studying is that studying aims to deepen understanding and gain mastery of a subject through systematic and purposeful engagement with the content. In this regard, Jesus in John 5:39 told the Pharisees, "*Search the scriptures; for in them ye think ye have eternal life: and they are they which testify of me."* Look at the word he used, "search," another befitting word for the activities described above, as studying. We often use "read" interchangeably with "study" in informal contexts to imply engagement with books in an attempt to comprehend information. It appears to me that this is the case here when we describe our use of the Bible as reading instead of studying, which is the most accurate thing to say.

Before I ever considered writing this book, one verse seemed to echo in my mind every time I discussed the essential steps to understanding the Bible—2 Timothy 2:15. It wasn't just a reference; it felt like an anchor, a guiding light; or at the very least, an unshakable memory verse. Back then, I read the scripture but hadn't fully grasped the weight of studying it as a crucial key to unlocking the true message of God's Word. Yet, no matter how much I tried to move past it, this verse refused to fade, pulling me back like a persistent whisper I couldn't ignore.

In 2 Timothy 2:15, the Apostle says, *study to shew thyself approved unto God, a workman that needeth not to be ashamed, rightly dividing the word of truth.* At first, I was concerned that the word "study" in this verse was unnecessarily distracting me because I could not just use a verse from the Bible to back up my action; I had to be sure of what the Bible says to make a doctrine or an actionable lesson from it. I had learned from so many preachers in the past that 2 Timothy 2:15 had nothing to do with studying the Bible. So, I keep clearing my mind each time the verse comes up during discussions. But I never stopped wondering: does this 'study' reference the Bible? So, the question is, does it refer to reading the Bible in any manner? I embarked on a study of 2 Timothy 2:15 and found the truth myself, alas! Yes, in a nutshell, it refers to the act of searching the Bible, but we will take a closer examination to grasp it in detail.

Remember that the person receiving the instruction is the author's student; in other words, it was an instructor's admonition to his student. Timothy, therefore, is being instructed by the phrase, "Study to show yourself approved," meaning he must learn what is necessary to gain approval. Consider students pursuing professional nursing, medicine, law, or teaching degrees. Not only must they pass their courses to graduate, but they also need to demonstrate competence by passing licensure exams. To succeed in these exams, they must acquire essential knowledge, which requires dedicated study using all available resources, books, lectures, or flashcards. Suppose we place this analogy side by side with the instruction in 2 Timothy 2:15. It'll be clear that, first, Paul's "show yourself approved" implies demonstrating competence. Second, the Scripture is a learning resource for Timothy, the books. The reader needs to know that this instruction applies not only to Timothy at that time but also to all of us who are now reading the message, as we must demonstrate our competence to God through studying His Word.

Someone may argue that the instruction could not have been connected to the Bible because it did not exist then; therefore, listing it as a learning resource for Timothy is wrong. In response to that, I'll show you what Paul said about Timothy in 2 Timothy 3:15, which states, *And that from a child thou hast known the holy scriptures, which are able to make thee wise unto salvation through faith which is in Christ Jesus.* It is clear from the above that the young Timothy has been studying the scripture. Paul may have checked him off as a performing student, but he must still demonstrate his competence with God. We need to understand from this illustration that the word study also means studying the Bible. Therefore, the Bible must be studied to be understood. We will build many of our discussions in this book on this verse because it is deeper than mere information to read and move on. We can see that the question of how we read the Bible, as asked by Jesus in Luke 10:26, seen above, lies in this verse. Recall that we mentioned that Jesus' question, "How do you read it?" also implies that the way (how) we read the scripture matters. To be clear, how we read the scripture determines how we understand it, as already hinted, meaning that if we read the right way, we get the right understanding and vice versa. Now that we've established, we must study the Bible. The key question is: how should we read it in a way that truly reflects studying?

The right way to read the Bible is to read it like a textbook. Before we delve into this point, let us examine the steps involved in reading or studying any book to understand the content better. We must read the words we see, not skip any, ignore any, paraphrase them, or assume other words could be better than any choice of words seen in any book passage. For example, 'how do you read it' should not be misplaced for 'how do you understand it' or how do you interpret it? Even when you believe the meanings are the same. This recommendation is very basic, and we will return to it later.

While we read the very words we see, we must follow all the rules used in reading, paying close attention to punctuation, such as commas, full stops, semicolons, colons, question marks, and parentheses. It is important to observe their use and purpose in each sentence. Usually, a period or full stop (.) is used to mark the conclusion of a phrase. A comma (,) separates clauses, phrases, and items in a list. A question mark (?) denotes an interrogative sentence. An exclamation point (!) is a punctuation mark that conveys intense emotion or emphasizes a statement. The colon (:) introduces a list, explanation, or quotation. A semicolon (;) is used to link closely related independent phrases. A dash (—) is utilized to emphasize, indicate a pause in thought, or separate a parenthetical statement. A hyphen (-) connects words or parts of words. An apostrophe (') indicates possession or the deletion of letters in contractions. Quotation marks, either in the form of double quotes (" ") or single quotes (' '), are used to indicate spoken language or titles of shorter works. Parentheses, sometimes called round brackets (()), enclose additional material or asides.

Observing these while reading any material clarifies what is read, including the Bible. Most times, people, out of emotion, forget to pay attention to punctuation when they read the Bible; when that happens, they run into errors. For example, read Matthew 5:18, A and B only, "*For verily I say unto you Until the heaven and the earth pass away...*". Now read Matthew 5:18, A and B, this time without the punctuation between you and until. "For verily I say unto you until the heaven and the earth pass away..." The two sentences do not communicate the same thing. The first, broken by a comma, says, "I tell you the truth, heaven, and earth can end, " In contrast, the second, with the omitted comma, says, "I'll continue to tell you the truth until heaven and earth end." The short exercise confirms how we can run into an erroneous interpretation just by ignoring the punctuation used in bible sentences.

Let's take a moment to briefly discuss commas, colons, and semicolons in breaking up clauses, as often seen in biblical texts. When a clause offers additional information or explanation about a previous clause, a comma is used, especially when the explanatory clause is nonrestrictive. For instance, in Psalm 23:1, *"The Lord is my shepherd, I shall not want,"* the comma separates the two clauses with "I shall not want," clarifying the first, emphasizing the result of God being one's shepherd.

A colon can introduce an explanation, often preceding a more detailed elaboration or clarification of the initial idea. This usage is common in the Bible, as seen in John 14:6: *"Jesus saith unto him, I am the way, the truth, and the life: no man cometh unto the Father, but by me."* Here, the phrase "no man cometh unto the Father, but by me" explains why Jesus is referred to as "the way, the truth, and the life" in the first clause.

The semicolon also appears several times in scripture, to connect related yet independent clauses that are too distinct for a comma but do not warrant a period. For example, in Matthew 21:13: *"And said unto them, It is written, My house shall be called the house of prayer; but ye have made it a den of thieves,"* the semicolon separates two independent clauses, each conveying a separate but related idea.

These are just a few instances of how punctuation marks function in the Bible. I encourage readers to explore the diverse uses of these punctuations further, as understanding their role is crucial to gaining accurate insight into the messages conveyed in the scripture

Someone may argue that punctuations in the Bible aren't important since they are not found in the original language from which the English versions are translated. The truth is, as languages differ, their use differs. It could probably be easier to understand where to end phrases and sentences in those other languages without punctuation; the tone or meanings communicated so far could suffice. But not so in English; punctuation is vital and primarily determines the meaning of sentences. Again, languages differ; in some languages, the tone of a word determines its meaning; a word can mean four different things depending on the tone used in saying it, just like the context of usage in a sentence can determine the meaning of a word in English. Since we are not writing a linguistic book, we do not intend to dwell on the language structure. We only need to drive a point home: God, who wants to communicate to us through the Bible, plans to do so in the way we communicate within ourselves, and therefore, we should apply the reading strategies we use in every other course material we read. When we say the Bible needs to be read or studied just like our textbooks, it is in this sense. Your goal should be to have the Bible speak to you after completing every verse.

Now that we have established that we should study the Bible like our textbooks, the next question is, how do we examine our textbooks? Of course, it would be wrong to assume that everyone reading this book must have read a textbook or have a reading strategy. When we read textbooks, we do not simply read passively but actively interact with the material. The process of studying may include discussion, analysis, synthesis, problem-solving, reflection, questioning, or any other method or combination that helps.

Let's discuss each of these manners of study in detail. Note, the study methods listed here are not in order of how they are to be applied, for example, questioning could be the first to be used when studying a verse before even discussion. Also, note that we must not utilize all of these strategies to understand every time we read. Some materials may require only one manner of study, while some may need us to employ more strategies. We may be required to switch from one study method to another or combine methods to understand the material. However, it is never mandatory to utilize any of these while studying. When we read our Bible like any other book, certain sentences or statements may be clear, straightforward, or self-explanatory. Those materials, therefore, need to be consumed without further juggling. For example, when we read statements like, '*In the beginning God created the heaven and the earth.*' (Genesis 1:1). A statement like the above does not require further efforts to understand that the Bible claims God brought our world into existence. One reading a clear statement as this could only further his understanding by asking how and why, which are the study strategies we described as questioning.

The first study strategy we mentioned was discussion. Discussion involves discussing the material with others, which could be with friends and family, study groups, or even a teacher. What discussion does is reinforce our understanding and expose us to different perspectives. Most times, readers tend to take discussion as their last studying step when they may have formed opinions on what they read. Most readers utilize it to develop or broaden their view for further scrutiny.

We also mentioned analysis, which is breaking down the information into smaller parts to understand it better. When the student analyzes, he might examine the components, identify patterns, or compare and contrast ideas. That is when most students read the same topics from different authors to fully grasp the concept under scrutiny.

Another strategy we mentioned was synthesis; in this case, different pieces of information are combined to create a new understanding. It's like putting together a puzzle, where each piece contributes to the whole picture.

Problem-solving is another study strategy that uses knowledge to solve issues or answer questions. It helps the student understand how the material can be applied in real-world circumstances.

Reflection is another way of studying and is the process of thinking about what you've learned and how it applies to your own experiences or views. It broadens your awareness and facilitates connections.

Questioning is another, asking questions about the material clarifies confusion and encourages further exploration. It demonstrates interest and an active desire to comprehend.

Lastly, practice entails repeatedly applying what is learned to strengthen understanding and enhance skills. It could include conducting exercises, solving issues, or even teaching the information to others.

In summary, approach studying the Bible as you would prepare for high school or college exams—with focus and intention. By applying the methods discussed above, the words of the Bible will begin to make sense and speak clearly. Once the Bible starts speaking through the studied pages, the next step is interpreting the words that resonate. This stage involves forming understanding, shaping beliefs, or even developing doctrine. It raises the crucial question: should the meaningful passages be taken literally, or do they carry symbolic meanings? This question will be explored in the next chapter.

4

LITERAL OR FIGURATIVE

Take every word of the Bible literally. We have repeatedly stated that the Bible is God speaking to us, and if God speaks to us, He conveys a message that needs to be understood at our level of understanding. Our level of understanding entails how we talk to ourselves; in other words, God intends to communicate with us in the same way we communicate with one another. Therefore, the Bible cannot speak in codes or hidden languages that must be decoded. Let's assume you enter a meeting with a few stakeholders in a company where you are meant to invest your life savings, and everyone in the meeting speaks slang language to the point that you do not fully grasp the outcomes of the meeting. But at the end of the meeting, everyone shook hands and left with smiles. Would you go ahead to invest your hard-earned money in that company? You would not, despite the excitement on the faces of the attendees.

Unfortunately, that is how most people read the Bible. Most readers read without understanding the message because they do not know how to render the words literally or otherwise. But again, the Bible should be read and understood literally, which is how we speak to each other in our day-to-day endeavors. When you read from Romans 8:1, *Therefore, there is now no condemnation for those who are in Christ Jesus*, it is just as literal as it reads: those who are in Christ Jesus are free from any sort of condemnation. When you read a text or sentence like this from the scripture, you only need to grasp it at its face value. If I am in Christ, then I am free from any form of condemnation. Similarly, when you read John 3:16, *For God so loved the world, that he gave his only begotten Son, that whosoever believeth in him should not perish, but have everlasting life*. The message is straightforward. God loves the world so much and gave his son to die for the world. The same is true when you read Acts 16:31: *"And they said, Believe on the Lord Jesus Christ, and thou shalt be saved, and thy house."* The message understood in the literal form is that they told the man that when he believes in the Lord Jesus Christ, he will be saved, and his household will be saved. There is no coded meaning, spiritual meaning, or biblical language in the sentences read.

The suggestion to render the ideas read from the Bible in the literal form may make some readers uncomfortable, especially when you are aware of some issues that have come up regarding the literal understanding of the word of God. A good example is the case of Galileo Galilei, who was "vehemently suspected of heresy" despite having sufficient empirical evidence that the Earth moves and that the Sun remains stationary at the center of the universe. He was believed to have held and defended an opinion even after it was said to be against Holy Scripture. It was so believed because the then catholic church read and rendered Joshua 10:13 literally, *"And the sun stood still, and the moon stayed until the people had avenged themselves upon their enemies."* A literal rendering of this verse to them at the time contradicted Galileo's scientific findings, which he vehemently defended against the then-powerful Roman Catholic. But truly, there is no conflict in ideas between the literal interpretation of Joshua 10:13 and the Scientists' findings. The conflict resulted, however, from the failure of the two parties to recognize their boundaries and their Jurisdiction.

When the Bible speaks of the sun, the idea is of the layman's sun, not the scientific sun. When the Bible speaks of the moon, not the scientific moon but the layman's moon. There is a difference between how the layman sees the sun and how the scientist sees it. When the layman sees the sun and the moon, he sees rays of light that we experience on our earth, whereas the scientist considers the sun a planetary body that illuminates our earth. So, when the Bible says that the sun moves, it simply says that the rays of light we experience move. Of course, it moves; it rises in the morning and sets in the evening. Rising and setting are movements of the rays of light, the sun, as we observe them on the Earth. This idea is completely different from saying that the planet Sun moves.

A practical guide to scriptural clarity

The church has not seen the heavenly bodies of which the sun is part, but has seen the rays of light everyone enjoys. The scientist was not speaking of the rays of light that the Bible speaks of, which the then church understood, but spoke of the planetary bodies he observed with his telescope, which is stationary. Again, the Bible is not a science book; it is not a geography book nor a book on astrology. The Bible is a father's note for his children; he will, therefore, speak to them in the language they will understand, in other words, how they communicate. This is important to note because someone may wonder why God, who made all these things and knows them all, decides to communicate with us in a manner that leaves a gap for conflicting scientific discoveries. Therefore, the issue of the church and the scientist in the seventeenth century is a boundary and jurisdiction issue, not how the Bible is rendered.

Our argument so far is that Bible phrases and sentences must be taken or understood literally as much as possible. However, there are situations when the words and sentences would not make sense when taken literally. In such situations, we are allowed to interpret figuratively. In short, the suggestion is to render the sentences or phrases of the Bible figuratively when the literal translation is illogical.

Imagine a reader encounters the term "clean heart" while reading Psalm 72. To understand its meaning, the reader might investigate the concept of a clean heart. If they were to interpret the term "heart" in this context as the physical, scientific heart—the organ that pumps blood through the body—they would misunderstand the passage, as the Bible is not a scientific textbook. Instead, the term "heart" in this biblical context could refer to a person's mind or inner being. Just as we regularly use the word "heart" to mean the mind or intention, such as in phrases like "follow your heart" or "he has a good heart," the term is still distinct from the scientific, anatomical heart, which is cardiac. Two things we must take from the above example: first, the heart is figurative, as we commonly use it. Second, the example further illustrates this distinction between the disciplinary realms of science and the Bible, an issue we discussed above.

Rest assured, the Bible is rich with figures of speech. Suppose God communicates with us through Scripture, like we naturally communicate with one another. It stands to reason that He, too, employs figurative expressions—just as we do in our everyday speech. We use figures of speech to make our conversation clearer, vivid, and emphatic. Making pictures, expressing feelings, and improving conversation can make writing more interesting, detailed, and memorable. Using figures of speech can also help make difficult thoughts easier to understand. A good example of the figure of speech in the Bible is Jesus' statement in Matthew 7:16, *Ye shall know them*

A practical guide to scriptural clarity

by their fruits. Taken literally, this statement would make little sense, as the act of bearing or producing fruit is exclusive to plants, not humans. Yet, Jesus explicitly attributes this action to people. He was employing a metaphor, illustrating that just as a tree is identified by the fruit it bears, a person's true nature is revealed by their actions and character. His use of metaphor substituted humans for plants. Recognizing this metaphorical substitution is crucial to grasping the meaning of the passage. This highlights the importance of understanding figures of speech in biblical interpretation, as Matthew 7:16 is far from the only instance where metaphors or other figures of speech are employed. In other words, a foundational knowledge of the language used in your Bible version is essential for a good understanding of Scripture. But do not be discouraged—there is good news ahead.

The good news is that the Bible has been translated into nearly every language humanity speaks. If the English version presents challenges requiring deeper linguistic skills, you can refer to a translation in a more familiar language for clarity. Additionally, there is no shortage of resources available to help sharpen language skills, making it easier to navigate and comprehend the Scriptures without unnecessary obstacles.

Another good example of a metaphor used by our lord is in John 15:5, *I am the vine, ye are the branches.* Again, he substituted himself and the believers with plants. To grasp this statement metaphorically, one must grasp the relationship between the characters, the plant, and the branches. For example, how does a branch relate to the tree again in layman's understanding? The branch stays glued to the tree to stay alive or survive. From that, we can grasp that the Savior speaks of him being our source, while we need to keep abiding and depending on him to remain relevant.

The Bible interestingly contains numerous figures of speech besides metaphor; look at some examples.

Simile: *for your goodness is as a morning cloud, and as the early dew it goeth away* (Hosea 6:4).

Metaphor: *I am the vine, ye are the branches* (John 15:5).

Personification: *Let the rivers clap their hands, let the mountains sing together for joy* (Psalm 98:8).

Hyperbole: *If your right eye causes you to sin, gouge it out and throw it away. For you should lose one of the parts of your body than for your whole body to be thrown into hell* (Matthew 5:29).

Paradox: *Whoever finds his life will lose it, and whoever loses his life for my sake will find it* (Matthew 10:39).

Anthropomorphism: *I will go down now, and see whether they have done altogether according to the cry of it, which is come unto me; and if not, I will know* (Genesis 18:21).

Synecdoche: *I am the good shepherd: the good shepherd giveth his life for the sheep* (John 10:11) and so many others. Identifying and understanding each of the figures of speech used is central to grasping the meaning of what we read from the Bible.

In summary, what we have said in this chapter is to read and understand the phrases and sentences of the Bible literally and figuratively when the literal reading does not make any sense. The outcome of doing so is that the readings of the Bible will begin to make logical sense to the reader, which will pave the way for understanding the doctrines buried between the lines. Let us end the chapter by echoing this: look for the figure of speech used in the Bible when it does not make literal sense.

5

RULES OF BIBLE INTERPRETATION

Bible interpretation is governed by certain rules, just as there are rules in other life events. We know that almost all the events of this life are governed by rules and regulations; in the same manner, some rules guide the interpretation of the Bible. Life without rules ends in chaos, and the same applies in our bid to understand the word of God. Many of the heretic messages and misleading doctrines circulating in the world today spring from not following the rules for Bible interpretation. So, Jesus' question found earlier in this book about how we read the scripture also entails whether we read with the rules.

But you may be wondering already about who made the rules. It appears to me that the author or the inspirer of the Bible, God, also gave certain rules to ensure anyone who reads it interprets it the correct way to obtain the same message. Theologians did not create these rules, but they study them. They might have developed numerous additional rules that are studied as the rules for interpreting the Bible. However, any rules may be useless when the Bible does not back them. *Except the LORD build the house, They labor in vain that build it:*

A practical guide to scriptural clarity

Except the LORD keep the city, The watchman waketh but in vain (Psalm 127:1).

Only the author of a document has a wholesome view of the content and meanings behind each phrase and is, therefore, the best person to explain how it should be read and interpreted. For this reason, some writers use their book launch occasions to summarize the key points they want readers to take away from their work or guide those who would read the book. So, any rules that people make will only help the reader understand the Bible from the point of view of that person.

However, the Bible needs to be interpreted from God's point of view. Because of this, it is very important to understand it using the rules and instructions that God himself made. Note the words of Jesus in John chapter 16 verse 13:

Howbeit when he, the Spirit of truth, is come, he will guide you into all truth: for he shall not speak of himself; but whatsoever he shall hear, that shall he speak: and he will shew you things to come.

This reinforces the argument that only the author of the Bible can provide the guidance needed to interpret it. On this note, the rules to be discussed or shown to you in this book are only those backed by the scripture, and those will be sufficient in your journey of understanding the words and will of God as written in the Bible.

Let the Scripture interpret the Scripture. This is the first rule for bible interpretation we will discuss. As earlier affirmed, this rule is backed by the Bible. In 1 Corinthians 2:13, we read, *These things we also speak, not in words which man's wisdom teaches but which the Holy Spirit teaches, comparing spiritual things with spiritual* (NKJV). We know that the messages of the Bible are spiritual, and we compare them with the words of the Bible, which are again spiritual. We, therefore, cannot interpret the scripture with wisdom from any other sources than the Bible, nor can we interpolate our earthly lifestyle into interpreting the Bible. This also relates to our discussion later in this chapter, the interpretation of the Bible from our shared experiences, events, or knowledge, which we shall address.

Many have fallen into erroneous and false ideas depending on any of these sources outside the Bible. Let us use one example to demonstrate how this law is utilized. Suppose you read Romans 8 verse 1, *There is therefore now no condemnation to them which are in Christ Jesus, who walk not after the flesh, but after the Spirit.* Then you may wonder who those 'in Christ Jesus' are or what it means to be 'in Christ Jesus' to be free from condemnation. If one tries to analyze this part of the Bible using common sense, experience, or knowledge, one could imply that "in Christ Jesus" is a kind of association or gathering such that membership releases the member from condemnation. Though this idea sounds decent and convincing, it is wrong, and another fellow may read it this way and attempt to further justify it by saying that the association is a Christian church or in Christendom, such that belonging to the Christian community is what it means to be in Christ. Whereas, to grasp the term "being in Christ Jesus," the reader needs to compare spiritual things with spiritual, as we described previously. This means comparing the bible verse in review with another bible verse to understand the term. In this regard, let us juxtapose Romans 8:1, stated above, with 2 Corinthians 5:17, which reads:

Therefore if any man be in Christ, he is a new creature: old things are passed away; behold, all things are become new.

We can see how the later verse defines the term 'in Christ Jesus', stating that the person in Christ is anyone born again. In other words, those in Christ are those who are born again. Therefore, to fully understand what Romans 8:1 means, we may compare it with 2 Corinthians 5:17 and infer that those born again are not condemned. This may be an easy fix for so many readers, but there are certainly more challenging and sophisticated ones in the Bible. Comparing the bible with the bible is key to clearing any uncertainty or defining difficult terminology in the Bible.

To further clarify our position in the example above, some may wonder what exactly distinguishes being born again from being in Christendom in our example above. Well, one can be in the church from birth to death without being born again. Many big names in the church today may miss the mark of our calling because of this issue. Most of them are born in the church and raised on Bible principles of morality. They, therefore, have no encounter with rebirth and rely on their morality. This can also be said about those who are raised in a Christian-dominated locality, who are Christians as a social standard, with no rebirth experience. That cleared, the point we have established is that we should use the bible to interpret the bible.

No scripture is interpreted in isolation. This is the second rule we must remember while reading and interpreting the Bible. We have seen how we should compare scripture with scripture to decipher the intent of God in every unclear portion read or to define terminologies; this second rule is another dimension of comparing scripture with scripture, but this time not to get clarification but to justify or solidify a point. This law of non-isolated portion interpretation also mandates the comparison before establishing a doctrine. The rule is according to 2 Peter 1:20, *Knowing this first, that no prophecy of Scripture is of any private interpretation, for prophecy never came by the will of man, but holy men of God spoke as they were moved by the Holy Spirit* (NKJV). Before establishing this point, let us also obey it by comparing and supplementing it with Second Corinthians

13:1: *This is the third time I am coming to you. In the mouth of two or three witnesses shall every word be established.* No only one individual carries a doctrine or message of the Bible. The same Holy Spirit who spoke to and through one prophet or minister speaks to and through another and, by so doing, conveys the same messages in diverse tones. This was one of the key decision criteria of canonization, as we have previously seen. Therefore, before you form any opinion of what you read from the Bible, ensure you have seen other portions with the same or a similar message. Take another example with Romans 8:1, which we have been studying. We earlier concluded that the verse means "there is no condemnation to individuals born again." Now, how can we boldly say this is what the bible says? Can we believe it is a biblical doctrine?

To conclude that this is what the bible is saying, we must find another portion that has the same or similar idea according to the second rule of bible interpretation. The verse that says the same thing is John 3:18. It reads- *He that believeth on him is not condemned: but he that believeth not is condemned already, because he hath not believed in the name of the only begotten Son of God.* We already know that believing makes us born-again; therefore, these two verses express the same: Born-again people are not condemned, so we can say, "This is what the bible says." I must say here that the examples we have used

How to understand the Bible

above are easy to follow, just for easy illustration's sake. Still, you might encounter more challenges while studying the bible daily, especially for a new reader. The difficulty lies in readily recalling any other verse with a similar idea and applying these principles learned when confronted with certain difficult chapters or verses. Remember, it is not a time to fold up and fall back on traditional ideas. Also, remember there is a need to read the bible for yourself. When identifying a complementary cum comparable bible portion becomes challenging, or maybe the reader is still a novice, the use of a study Bible becomes instrumental.

Most study Bibles are structured to help readers easily connect to other bible portions with similar ideas. The cross-referencing tool in Study Bibles could be utilized to see how different parts of the Bible connect and support each other regarding specific concepts or doctrines. Another helpful tool in the Study Bible used in this regard is the Topical Index or concordance, which could be used to find verses and passages related to specific doctrines, allowing for a comprehensive view of what the Bible teaches on a particular topic. In addition, the study bible includes additional resources, including the commentary and explanations, as well as the charts and maps. You can quickly glance at the commentary sections to observe how other scholars interpret or explain the intricate doctrines you are examining and the theologians' perspectives. The charts and maps are visual aids that can improve our comprehension of the development and context of biblical doctrines throughout history, as well as the timelines of the Bible. Although these tools can help facilitate your understanding of the bible since humans design them, they should not be taken as absolute; you must discern as you use them to study. As you continue to read the Bible, you will accumulate more of this complementary correspondence of bible portions. Once these messages are stored in your soul, they will be recalled. It appears that the Holy Spirit is the one who assists the believer in recollecting this information. We will discuss the reasons for this later.

Furthermore, this no-interpretation-in-isolation rule also highlights the need for the lessons we learn from our reading to be consistent with the larger framework of the Bible's teachings. As a result, no interpretation of one verse should conflict with another or with the overall message of the Bible. For example, some people have misinterpreted Genesis 4:16-17 by claiming that there were other people on earth before Adam and Eve, as evidenced by Cain finding a wife. However, this assumption is incorrect because it contradicts Genesis 2:7, which clearly states that Adam and Eve were the first humans created by God. Therefore, it is not sufficient to read a single portion of the Bible and proceed with it; rather, there must be another portion that conveys a similar concept for your comprehension to be considered a doctrine, and the doctrine formed must align with the overall message of the bible.

Speak where the Bible speaks and be silent where the Bible is silent is the third rule for bible interpretation that demands our attention if we must understand the words of God. In other words, only say what the bible says. It was a popular phrase that came to light in the restoration movement, an event we will not narrate in this book. Still, this rule emphasizes following the Bible explicitly and not adding to its teachings. It is not intended to be if it is not in the bible. Flawing this principle could be obvious when people completely say what the bible did not state, or subtly when they add a few words or phrases. Again, it can happen in various ways, but the most prevalent way it occurs is the addition of words to the words of the Bible, which we will dedicate a chapter to.

Other than that, people make assertions that are not in the bible and convincingly believe those are the words of God. For example, people often say, "Heaven help those who help themselves." Some people genuinely feel they are quoting scripture when they use this line, even though it does not appear anywhere in the Bible. By His purpose for us, our flawless God has given us faultless words that are complete, accurate, and comprehensive. The sweet-sounding ideas you assume should be in His words are probably not his will towards us. But before we dive into this conversation fully, let us pause and ask if the bible asks us to be vocal where it is and silent where it is. Proverbs 30:5-6 interestingly said so, *Every word of God is pure: He is a shield unto them that put their trust in him. Add thou not unto his words, Lest he reprove thee, and thou be found a liar.* Just to be very clear, when you speak about God or His words and choose to speak anything that is not mentioned in the Bible, God considers you a liar. It's that simple.

The author of Hebrews utilized this rule in Hebrews 13:5-6, *"Let your conversation be without covetousness; and be content with such things as ye have: for he hath said, I will never leave thee, nor forsake thee. So that we may boldly say, The Lord is my helper, and I will not fear what man shall do unto me"*. Now let's take a second to demonstrate this. If you remove some words in verses 5 and 6 just for this illustration, we will have "He has said…so that we may boldly say… What would you consider this? I see this as speaking where He speaks or where the bible speaks. Again, in 2 John 9-11, the bible said that if any man should come to you in the name of God without standing on the doctrine of Christ, do not give credence to such a one. 2 Corinthians 2:17, Lamentations 3:37-38 are all illustrations of speaking only the words of God. Lastly, in 1 Corinthians 4:6, the Holy Spirit warned us against using the words of men as authorities rather than relying only on the written words. Whoever says or writes about God, if the Bible does not support it, then their statement is a falsehood according to the judgment of God. This is true regardless of who is speaking or writing. I wish these twenty-first-century believers would use the instruction in this paragraph to sieve all the 'God said to me' they hear in their congregations week after week; they would wake up and search for the true and invisible God, the Father of our Lord Jesus Christ.

Let us look at some concrete examples of not being mute in situations where the Bible is silent. When people suggest that there were many people on earth before Adam and Eve, as mentioned in the example above, an assumption that arises because the Bible does not provide details about the background of Cain's wife in Genesis 4:16-17 is a concrete example to start with. Have you heard the story of how Satan disobeyed God when he was sent on an errand? You can never find a thing like that in the Bible, which is a typical example of not stopping where the bible stopped.

The only account of Lucifer turning into Satan and being cast out from heaven was in Isaiah 14:12-14, where he wanted to assume an authoritative position like his creator God. How about the assumption that Satan takes permission from God before he tempts a believer? This is another subtle statement made out of violating this rule that is widely believed today. Only recently did I notice that popular sayings such as "God works in mysterious ways" and "Cleanliness is next to Godliness" are never in the Bible, after I read it from a write-up online. Another example is the pleasant-sounding mess made out of Proverbs 16:18, "Pride goes before a fall," which is not what the bible says. However, you can read from the Bible: *"Pride goeth before destruction, and a haughty spirit before a fall"* (Proverbs 16:18).

I believe that no two English words are the same; if they were, there wouldn't be a need to invent the second. We cannot, therefore, say haughtiness is the same as pride. To understand this perspective, the sin of Satan, as described in Isaiah 14:12-14, which caused his fall, is a perfect description of a haughty spirit spoken about in Proverbs 16:18. We need to report what the bible records and refrain from rephrasing it and adding our ideas to sound good to ourselves. It would never be His Word if it were not from the Word.

Read the Bible in context; in other words, read and comprehend the Bible messages in their context. This is the fourth rule of bible interpretation we need to follow. In Proverbs 18:13, the bible says, *He that answereth a matter before he heareth it, it is folly and shame unto him.* In essence, reading in context is very important, and concluding a point without or before completely understanding the context is akin to responding to a matter before hearing it. We can further illustrate contextual reading with the account of the Ethiopian Eunuch, and Philip found in Acts 8:30-34, paying close attention to the Eunuch's question in verse 34. *And the eunuch answered Philip, and said, I pray thee, of whom speaketh the prophet this? of himself, or of some other man?*

Simply put, the eunuch asked Phillip to explain the context of the passage he was reading. He was fully convinced of the message as soon as he grasped the context of what he read, as evidenced by his conversion, which became seamless as soon as he comprehended the context of the passage. Another lesson we can learn from this illustration is that the appropriate response to God's word is contingent upon its thorough understanding. Comprehending its context often facilitates this, and we will see more of this in the coming pages.

Reading out of context is like a motorist traveling to an unknown destination following the direction of a global positioning system (GPS) device without adhering to the entire direction the GPS provides. When the traveler stopped at a set of lights, he heard the GPS, for example, say, "At the next light, turn right." But because the driver didn't pay attention to the entire sentence or the context, he turned right where he was standing, which caused him to lose his path. Although the driver followed the GPS's instructions to turn right, the timing of the turn was defined in the context, which wasn't instantaneous.

Let us look at some vital examples of Bible verses taken out of context. 1 Timothy 6:10 is the Bible verse people often quote wrong because they don't read the context. When people don't read and understand the Bible in its proper context, they usually do it in paragraphs or chapters. But in this case, it's a single phrase: *For the love of money is the root of all evil: which while some coveted after, they have erred from the faith, and pierced themselves through with many sorrows* (1 Timothy 6:10).

People often say, "Money is the root of all evil." No, that is not what the bible says. If one verse in the Bible asserts that money is the root of all evil, and then in another portion states that "money answereth all things" (Ecclesiastes 10:19), the Bible would contradict itself, speak ill of money, on the one hand, and speak well of money on the other hand. However, we know that the Bible can never contradict itself (Romans 3:4). Rather, reading the passage and considering the surrounding context will reveal that the love of money is what the Bible denounces. People simply read and take those readings out of context and misquote the bible in the earlier verses. Another example of reading taken out of context is Romans 8, verse 28. This one is very subtle, so it takes maximum attention to understand that it is taken out of context. People usually assert that it's all good, a blessing in disguise, or that every disappointment is a blessing. When you ask a bible student to back up any of these claims, like I once did, they will quickly cite this Bible verse, reading it as "all things work together for good." But that is not what the bible says. Pick up your bible and read the exact words of Romans 8:28. It reads, *And we know that all things work together for good to them that love God, to them who are the called according to his purpose.* Why would readers ignore the placement of a comma in the sentence? If readers had stopped where the comma is placed, which is the correct thing to do, the message would be complete, and nothing would have been taken out of context. As the context contained the person receiving the promise, we mean that the verse highlights persons for whom everything works together for their benefit. Whenever we apply this scripture to any person who is going through a challenging moment, we do so out of context, since it is possible that the verse may not apply to that individual. It would only apply to the person if the conditions outlined in that verse also apply to the individual. These qualifications include being a lover of God and being among those called by God and his purpose.

The point we are making here is that when we read, we should look at the bigger picture to understand the broad message or the undertone of what we are reading. It is important to always understand the context, since that will enable us to know if the passage is an analogy, an example, a command, or a statement.

Another question we will answer is whether it is ever right to use any verse out of context. Well, the answer is no; there is no time when taking the bible out of context is permitted or when it is a good practice, no matter how nice the out-of-context message may sound. When the word of God is taken out of context, the resulting message ceases to be the word of God but the word of man, who had taken it out of context. One can argue that since it is a cutout from the word of God, it remains the word of God since He has these pieces. But the truth is, if God intended to say that formulated from an off-context cut-out, there would not have been a need for the full passage or sentence from which it was extracted. A very good example to illustrate taking some of God's word out of context to create beautiful and attractive messages that do not fulfill God's will is that of a mother leaving her two children at home with a written note for the older one. On the note, she writes, 'I have left you twenty dollars; buy a cup of large fries and ice cream for your baby sister, and the remaining money is for anything you would like.' Upon reading the notes, the child became excited and only read the part that says, 'I have left you twenty dollars." Of course, she would enjoy whatever she buys with the twenty dollars that automatically becomes hers since she took the first phrase out of context. Still, she would never please the mom, who meant both children in her note. Because the child read the sentence and took the first phrase out of context, the word 'you' in the first phrase becomes singular rather than plural, which her mother intended. This is what it looks like when a reader takes any word or phrase of the bible out of context because it sounds interesting or inspiring; he ends up consuming sermons that are not God-breathed. It implies that we will never please God when we practice or act on the word that comes from reading His words out of context.

One of the best ways to get the context of a verse read from the bible is to start from the beginning of the chapter. That will at least tell you who the entire chapter is addressing and the tone of the message, which will also aid in its application. In most cases, however, we do not have to read the entire chapter or all the preceding verses all the time to understand the context. Reading a few verses ahead of the verse being examined can help to clarify the context.

Never interpret the bible with experience; this is the fifth rule of bible interpretation we will discuss. Please note that we can rather explain our experiences with the bible but cannot interpret the bible with our experience. Experiences are both relative and subjective. My personal experiences might differ from yours and are mostly influenced by my decisions. Therefore, experiences are not standardized and cannot be measured. In addition to that, God and his ways are bigger than our experiences. I heard a young man say that the Bible's warnings against sexual immorality only apply to married people. He said this because, as a young man, he tried to stay celibate but couldn't because of his sexual urges, even though he prayed to God many times to take them away. In the same

A practical guide to scriptural clarity

line of thought, a pastor backed his belief about generational curses on an experience he had on the passing of his dear friend. He said that he was worried about certain people in his friend's family dying in a certain way at a certain time or season. He told his friend about this worry, but his friend downplayed it by saying that if someone is in Christ, old things have passed. In the end, this friend died the same way his relatives did. So, he thought that some generational courses or agreements are not broken when a person is born again. These are the wrong ways to build doctrines. It must be the word explaining our experiences and not vice versa. Thirdly, I listened to an interview with a well-known preacher encouraging believers not to avoid divorce. In his own words, when attempting to answer a question about Malachi 2:16, which seems to contradict what he was saying. He stated that some of these works are no longer relevant in the present world. He offered examples of prominent preachers who had gone through divorces in their marriages and concluded that it should have been the will of God, as otherwise these men would not have gone through such happenings. Hearing this as his defense, I was greatly disappointed because the fact that these big men of God, so-called, went through it does not justify it, nor does it negate the viewpoint God holds on it.

The imperfection of men cannot nullify the reality of the word of God; therefore, it is very wrong and would be unfortunate to attempt to use fallible men's experiences to interpret the infallible word of God. For example, many have used the name of Jesus to perform many authentic and verifiable miracles, such as healing the sick and performing signs and wonders. Still, some others have died calling on the same name. That does not imply that the promise by the master in John 16:23-24 is false or belongs to certain individuals. Rather, we should understand that certain unobvious factors could have been responsible for the blockage of fulfilling these promises to certain individuals. When these shortcomings are absent in others, they obtain the breakthrough they seek. One's spiritual state is one of these unobvious factors that come into play, and unfortunately, we can only see one's actions but not their spiritual standing. It could surprise you that many who would argue they are born again today are not. How could they have obtained something God has reserved for His children? (Matthew 15:26). We must avoid using experiences to interpret the words we read from the bible.

Nevertheless, it is of the utmost importance to point out that our experiences might help us navigate towards the right knowledge of the word of God. For instance, if we have previously studied incorrect doctrines and have failed each time we have attempted to put them into practice, this may cause us to question whether or not what we have learned is exactly what the Bible teaches, which would then drive us to engage in some studies of the Bible. Revelational knowledge, which is information that brings us into another dimension of our faith and the knowledge of God, would be made possible as a result of the study. This final illustration demonstrates how the Bible can provide explanations for various phenomena that occur in life. For further clarification, the pastor who has lost a friend who passed away in the same manner as his ancestors have repeatedly passed away could simply reason that, despite the years he has spent in the ministry, his friend might have either not been born again yet or was still a baby believer without the knowledge of his sonship rights and privileges, which is a spiritual state that we are unable to see.

6

ADD NOT, SUBTRACT NOT

This may sound familiar already; of course, we have briefly touched on this topic while discussing the rules of Bible interpretation; it is so important, however, that we dedicate a whole chapter to deal with it in detail because it holds a big place in our journey of reading and understanding the scriptures. The Bible, both in the New and Old Testaments, continued to warn us against adding to or subtracting from its content. Deuteronomy 4:2 and Revelation 22:18-19 explicitly state these warnings:

Ye shall not add unto the word which I command you, neither shall ye diminish ought from it, that ye may keep the commandments of the Lord your God which I command you... If any man shall add unto these things, God shall add unto him the plagues that are written in this book: And if any man shall take away from the words of the book of this prophecy, God shall take away his part out of the book of life, and out of the holy city, and from the things which are written in this book.

Before establishing our position, we should know that the warnings are literal and should be taken seriously. Apart from heeding the warning, a serious student should ask why it is so important not to add or subtract from the words of the Bible. So important that some punishment is reserved for the violators. Recall that we have previously noted that once a word is added to that which is written, the message becomes the words of man, the one who added to the Bible, and that is what God wants to prevent, hence the statement... *that ye may keep the commandments of the Lord your God which I command you.* The implication is that once a word is added, you henceforth keep the commandment of the one who has altered the message and not heed the word of God, which is why it is important. God wants you to hear His voice each time you fasten your eye on the pages of the Bible. He wants a listener to hear His voice each time a verse is read out loud; that is a point we can establish from the first part of the above warning.

But that is not the only danger to be aware of; adding or subtracting from the word often derails the perception of the intended message. As previously discussed, this is the issue with most of the newest translations. When we looked into the various Bible versions, we listed Bible verses where some words found in the KJV are missing in some of the other Bible versions, especially the newer ones. We will, however, illustrate this further with another example. In Habakkuk 2 verse 4, some NIV versions almost derailed the meaning of the verse by introducing a word that is never meant to be there. The NIV translation's inclusion of the term "enemy" altered the verse's entire meaning, making it about God's faithfulness, whereas the verse is never about God's faithfulness but faith in Christ. It emphasizes that righteousness is attained through faith. This concept is echoed in Romans 1:17, which states, "*For therein* (in the gospel) *is the righteousness of God revealed from faith to faith: as it is written, 'The just shall live by faith.'*" These passages collectively convey that individuals transition from spiritual death to eternal life through faith, leading to justification and righteousness before God. In this context, "the just" refers to those deemed righteous, "live" signifies the awakening to eternal life, and "faith" pertains to belief in Christ. Thus, the essence of the gospel is encapsulated in the truth that the righteous obtain eternal life through faith in Christ. This message is hidden by introducing a word into a verse.

Once the message of the Bible is altered, what you get from the reading is nothing but an inaccurate understanding of the message, as demonstrated above. In logic, once the premises are wrong, the outcomes are wrong, and acting on the wrong conclusion is as good as obeying man rather than God, as we have seen above.

Experience has shown us that when people add to or diminish from the scripture, they often do so to win arguments or to prove points. This is a pitfall we must guard against. I remember a discussion with a pastor when I visited his church for a ministration. During our conversation, his wife initiated an interesting conversation about fashion and faith. After listening to him and another minister who accompanied me discuss the significance of being well-dressed, I disclosed that I did not have a personal opinion but relied solely on the scripture. I recited the keywords of 1 Peter 3:3 & 4 off-hand. I could recall I said, "Whose adorning let it not be that outward adorning, but let it be the hidden man of the heart." The pastor cut in and said, "You missed something." I replied, "What?" and he said, "That place says let it not ONLY be…" I was shocked because it's a verse I am familiar with. I responded, "I do not think there is ONLY in the phrase." His wife backed him up the same minute and said, "There is!" With no intention of arguing, I decided to be silent and quietly read the verse again with the Bible application on my phone, and lo! There is no 'ONLY' in the verse. No wonder she got it wrong and was worried about what she should not be worried about. They have erroneously inserted a word into what is written. For the benefit of the reader, 1 Peter 3:3-4 says, *Whose adorning let it not be that outward adorning of plaiting the hair, and of wearing of gold, or of putting on of apparel; But let it be the hidden man of the heart, in that which is not corruptible, even the ornament of a meek and quiet spirit, which is in the sight of God of great price.* We could infer from these verses that if you must admire a person, it must be based on the inward man; condemning a man also ought to be based on the inward man and not on outward appearance, which includes his dressing. So, when she inserted the word 'only' before the word 'be,' it changed the entire message. It turned her message to mean that several other considerations could be utilized to evaluate a person apart from the inward man. You could see that this wrong rendering allowed her to consider dressing as one of those other measures, which is not what the bible says. I do not advocate for indecent dressings, but let's be clear that Jesus did not die on the cross to fix our wardrobe. Secondly, we need to stop where the bible stopped.

Next time you pick up your Bible, approach it with an open mind, free from any preconceived notions, so you can avoid reading it into the text. Read only the words you see, seize meanings from the words you read, and consider linking their ideas with a previously learned concept afterward. Likewise, pick up yours and read along when you hear someone tell you what the bible says. This is why we encourage everyone to bring a copy to church so you can examine yourself, what you are taught, and what preachers are reading for you. If you can avoid adding or diminishing words of the bible, it would help you understand it the right way and improve your interpretation skills each time you read.

Another subtle way people subtract from the bible is by ignoring some words as if they are unimportant. We have previously established that every word in the bible is inspired, including the one our instinct downplays at certain moments. Downplaying the significance or completely ignoring that single word could alter the entire message of the verse. Let's look at this with an example. We have talked about one of the most loved verses of the bible before, *And we know that all things work together for good to them that love God, to them who are the called according to his purpose* (Romans 8:28). You will agree with me that most times when people quote this verse, they often end it halfway, "all things work together for good." Some will add "to them that love God" and end it there. Ending a bible verse halfway without completing at least a phrase where the comma is placed presents an incomplete message and is erroneous because all things do not always work together for the good of everyone. Also, reading a verse like this somehow demands reading and incorporating the whole idea. For example, if you stop after the first phrase, the message makes sense and would be correct, but incomplete, because loving God is not the only condition to be met. In other words, all the conditions required are not met by only loving God; you have to be 'the called' in addition to merit the blessing in the verse.

One more omission that I noticed most people make in this verse is the omission of 'the' before called. Most fellows recite it as…to them who are called according to his purpose. That changes the intention of specifying who the verse speaks about. It could surprise you that you may have been guilty of this particular act subconsciously. That is probably why this information is coming to you, and to be forewarned is to be forearmed. There was a verse that I fell victim to myself, although I would not describe myself then as a bible student. But I continued to retain this distorted information until it pleased the lord to reveal this studying strategy of ensuring every word is read to me, and I was seized in both awe and laughter. I have encountered countless folks with the same distorted information that I harbored for years, meaning that they had downplayed the same word I did when I was taught this bible verse. I know you must have heard Isaiah 54:17 quoted over and over again. Now pause and think how you have memorized it; if you did, now let's read it together. *No weapon that is formed against thee shall prosper; and every tongue that shall rise against thee in judgment thou shalt condemn. This is the heritage of the servants of the Lord, and their righteousness is of me, saith the Lord.* Many of us omit or downplay one word in this verse very often. The word 'thou' in the second clause of the statement is often not added when reciting this verse. We make it read, "and every tongue that shall rise against thee in judgment shalt be condemned." Now pause again: have you been quoting or reciting this verse as we have recounted in the recent quote? You are as guilty as I was. Do you know that omitting that word changed the meaning of the whole verse? It truncates the real message God is passing. We have continued to secure this incorrect rendering of that scripture because it assuages the desire of some ignorant Christians who rely on God for everything, including what He has given them the ability to accomplish. I mean, most of us have ignorantly believed that God will do everything for us, and we have nothing to do. Those in this circle, therefore, spiritualize everything about life. But when we read Isaiah 54:17 the way it is written without subtracting a word, it reads, *"and every tongue that shall rise against thee in judgment thou shalt condemn,"* we will then see a part we have to play, of course, with the ability of God, you have acquired at the new birth. You are to condemn every tongue that shall rise against you. Jehovah will not do it for you; you will! That is what the bible says. This shows how important it is to avoid subtracting from the Bible's words, intentionally or otherwise.

To conclude this chapter, we have emphasized the importance of reading the Bible with caution and ensuring that you read the words as they are written, without presuming that a word needs to be added or the significance of any word or words is diminished. Pay close attention to each word to comprehend the meaning of each phrase or sentence in the Bible. This will enhance your understanding of the message as a whole.

7

RIGHTLY DIVIDE

You might be tempted to skip this chapter because of the traditional way we've come to understand the phrase "rightly dividing." However, this chapter stirred my spirit into writing a book that unlocks the understanding of the scripture. In 2 Timothy 2:15, as we read earlier, the apostle Paul instructed Timothy to rightly divide the word of truth. The phrase rightly dividing, as used here, has been conventionally interpreted to mean 'correctly explaining' or 'properly interpreting.' These conventional representations may be right, but I am compelled to argue that there is more to it than these. Without much digging into the Greek word *tomounta*, which means to cut, used in 2 Timothy 2:15, let us acknowledge that words such as *diermēneusen* translated as expounded in Luke 24:27, which is from the verb *diermēneuō* which means 'to interpret,' 'to explain,' was available in the Greek language during the time 2 timothy 2:15 was written. *Diermēneusen* (interpret) could have been used instead of *tomounta* (cut) in that verse if the author intends to communicate the conventional interpretation given to the verse. But it pleases the Holy Spirit to use the word *tomounta*, cut, and by implication divide to communicate the exact thing, and one of the most important things we must do with the scripture. It appears to me, therefore, that the holy spirit wants us to cut the scripture or divide it while studying it.

The KJV translator's use of the word divide is perfect since when you cut an object, you divide it. When we cut or divide the scripture correctly, which is the instruction given to the young Timothy, we obtain God's approved message, which will never lead us astray and align with the rest of the scripture.

The Bible follows a timeline where events unfold in various times and seasons, often called eras. In each era, God interacts with individuals based on what is available. Let's clarify this point by referring to Hebrews 1:1-2, which says, *God, who at sundry times and in divers manners spake in time past unto the fathers by the prophets, Hath in these last days spoken unto us by his Son, whom he hath appointed heir of all things, by whom also he made the worlds.* The message should be clear by now: how God spoke to the fathers in the past differs from how He spoke to us in these last days. His son was not available to the fathers but available to us. Also, in Jeremiah 31:31-34, we can find how God changes his dealings with mankind from one generation to another. Jeremiah 31:31-34 reads, 31 *Behold, the days come, saith the Lord, that I will make a new covenant with the house of Israel, and with the house of Judah: 32 Not according to the covenant that I made with their fathers in the day that I took them by the hand to bring them out of the land of Egypt; which my covenant they brake, although I was an husband unto them, saith the Lord: 33 But this shall be the covenant that I will make with the house of Israel; After those days, saith the Lord, I will put my law in their inward parts, and write it in their hearts; and will be their God, and they shall be my people. 34 And they shall teach no more every man his neighbor, and every man his brother, saying, Know the Lord: for they shall all know me, from the least of them unto the greatest of them, saith the Lord: for I will forgive their iniquity, and I will remember their sin no more.*

First, it is noted that God established a covenant in the past, followed by a promise of a new covenant, after which an era would ensue in which the law would indwell the people of Israel. One can ask, what changes did he make here? In the first covenant, he was a husband; in the second, he became their God, indicating a change in His dealings and covenant type. We can infer that God adjusts His interactions with humanity to suit their evolving eras. Also, in Romans 2, the bible tells us that the law will be used to judge those who live under the law, but not so with those who lived before it, whose God's judgment would be according to their consciences. So, our era is an important determinant of how God deals with us. Therefore, when we rightly divide the scripture, we do so according to the different times on the biblical timeline or era the message falls on. Many Bible scholars use the term 'dispensations' to describe these eras, typically identifying seven. However, this book is not focused on theology but on helping readers develop the skills to understand and apply the Bible effectively. Therefore, we will focus only on the eras described, not on dispensations.

Jesus demonstrated this act of rightly dividing the scripture during his early public ministry. In Luke 4:14-30, Jesus took the scroll or the scripture and read Isaiah 61:1-2 to the people's hearing. He did not finish the whole of the second verse; he rather cut it in between and commented on what he read. For clarity, Isaiah 61:1-2 reads *"The Spirit of the Lord God is upon me; because the Lord hath anointed me to preach good tidings unto the meek; he hath sent me to bind up the brokenhearted, to proclaim liberty to the captives, and the opening of the prison to them that are bound; To proclaim the acceptable year of the Lord, and the day of vengeance of our God; to comfort all that mourn."* Now look at what Jesus read according to Luke 4:18 to 21 *"The Spirit of the Lord is upon me, because he hath anointed me to preach the gospel to the poor; he hath sent me to heal the brokenhearted, to preach deliverance to the captives, and recovering of sight to the blind, to set at liberty them that are bruised, To preach the acceptable year of the Lord. And he closed the book, and he gave it again to the minister...And he began to say unto them."*

Now, the big question is, why did Jesus stop reading at this point without reading to the end of a verse he had already started? Of course, you will agree that he never omitted it or missed it in error. He intentionally avoided reading the part…*and the day of vengeance of our God; to comfort all that mourn.* He stopped because the timing would be wrong, even though the whole verse talks about what he would do, the ending verse contains a future event that has not been fulfilled. Hence, he said…*This day is this scripture fulfilled in your ears* (verse 21b). Again, he decided to rightly divide what was written and only read what applied to him and the congregation at that moment: He couldn't have said that the scripture had been fulfilled if he had finished reading the whole verse, since that would contain some future and unfulfilled events.

We need to understand the different Bible eras, including the one we live in, and place events and books within their proper timelines. This helps us read Scripture accurately and apply only what is relevant to our era. Remember that while the scripture was written for us to learn, not all is intended for our practice. If we pay attention to the verse in Isaiah 61:1-2, which Jesus read in Luke 4:18-21, it contains useful information people need to know about the future events Jesus would accomplish. Still, He divided it to use what applies at the time of the reading only. We also need to do the same when we read the bible; we need to recognize these eras and divide what we read accordingly. Having established that we need to divide the bible into different eras, what are these eras along the bible timelines?

First, let's understand the Bible timeline and the flow of biblical events. The Bible timeline could be grouped as- Creation: The beginning of the world (Genesis 1–2), Patriarchal Period: The lives of the patriarchs—Abraham, Isaac, Jacob, and Joseph (Genesis 12–50).

Exodus and Conquest: The deliverance of Israel from Egypt and their conquest of Canaan (Exodus–Joshua).

Judges: The period of the judges leading Israel (Judges–1 Samuel).

United Kingdom: The reigns of Saul, David, and Solomon (1 Samuel–1 Kings).

Divided Kingdom: The division of Israel into the northern kingdom (Israel) and the southern kingdom (Judah) (1 Kings–2 Kings).

Exile and Return: The Babylonian exile and the return to Jerusalem (2 Kings, 2 Chronicles, Ezra, Nehemiah).

Intertestamental Period: The 400 years between the Old and New Testaments.

Life of Christ: The birth, ministry, death, and resurrection of Jesus (Matthew–John).

Early Church: The establishment and spread of the church accounts in Acts and Epistles.

End Times: The prophetic events described in Revelation. Note, however, that these timelines presented the flow of biblical events, which are not themselves the divisions we need to make. It will rather enable us to rightly divide. To rightly divide, we must divide the bible according to how God deals with humans in a given period along the discussed timeline. When we do that, five different eras will emerge, which include the pre-law era (without the law), the law era, the grace era (church age), the tribulation, and the millennial reign era (the kingdom). Then, we must find in the timeline where these eras are located.

We could suggest from the arranged timeline above that the Creation and the Patriarchal Period belong to the pre-law era. The Exodus and Conquest, Judges, United Kingdom, Divided Kingdom, Exile and Return, and Intertestamental Period belong to the law. The Early Church and some parts of the End Times belong to the grace, while some parts of the End Times belong to tribulation. This might not seem easy at first, but it becomes easier to understand and remember with practice. Remember that 2 Timothy 2:15 says you're truly a God-approved minister when you grasp these divisions and can apply them effectively.

Although we have successfully listed different timelines and placed them into the eras they may fall into, the biggest task is to realize exactly when they begin and end and where they fall into in the actual books. For example, we stated above that the law started in Exodus, but it did not until Moses received the commandment, an event described deep into the chapter. This means that the era we described as 'the pre-law' extended into Exodus. The trend continued in other eras mentioned.

When you flip through a copy of the 36-book Bible, one of the first things you'll notice is that it's divided into two main sections: the Old Testament and the New Testament. According to the arrangement of the books, the Old Testament ends in Malachi, while the New Testament starts with Matthew. Yet, this isn't the division we need to make to understand the bible the God's way. Therefore, we want to re-echo that the way to easily divide the Bible to facilitate revelational knowledge of the word of God easily is to divide it into five: before the law/ the law/ the grace/ the tribulation /the millennial reign. We also need to remember that each era commences where the preceding terminates. The division acknowledged as 'Before the law' or without the law (Romans 2:12) started from the creation of man in Genesis and mankind's early life in the garden of Eden and terminates in Exodus, after the giving and receiving of the Mosaic Law (Exodus 19–20), around 1446 BC. The second phase of the division is 'the law.' The law started in Exodus 19, upon receiving the law on Mount Sinai, as earlier stated, it ended when Jesus died on the cross. Yes, that was not a typo; the law did not end in Malachi as you may have expected, but on the cross. Colossians 2:14 makes this clear: *Blotting out the handwriting of ordinances that was against us, which was contrary to us, and took it out of the way, nailing it to his cross.* The cross, however, extends through the four Gospels, Matthew, Mark, Luke, and John. The law ends at the cross, while grace begins on the cross after the death and the resurrection of Jesus Christ (Hebrews 9:17), around AD 30–33. Since 'the Grace,' also known as the church era, began, we have been in it to date. The Grace will end at the second coming of Jesus Christ and will mark the beginning of the tribulation, while the millennial reign of Christ will begin as soon as the tribulation ends.

Having stated that the Grace era would end at the second coming of Jesus (1 Thessalonians 4:16-17), often described by a popular non-biblical term, the rapture. It is important to state that its time is unknown to us; it was not explicitly stated, and we therefore cannot guess; we ought to remain silent where the bible is silent. The rapture, otherwise the end of the grace era, will usher in the tribulation era (Matthew 24:21-22), and the end of the tribulation brings in a new era, the Millennial reign (Matthew 24:29-30). Again, we are still in the Grace era, the church age, not yet in the tribulation or the millennial reign.

Therefore, when we read the bible, we need to discover which era the message obtained falls into because we cannot practice the instructions that do not fall into the era of Grace simply because they were never made for us in this era. For example, we cannot begin to live by the things written under the law, which was never for us in this era, *for ye are not under the law, but under grace* (Romans 6:14 b). *For Christ is the end of the law for righteousness to every one that believeth* (Romans 10:4).

Unfortunately, millions of church attendees do not know this. I remember when one of my friends expressed her worries concerning the curse that may come upon her for not tithing. I was all smiles while listening to her narrate how not tithing would enable her to cover her fraction of the tuition needed to remain in school, but jeopardize her standing with God, in addition to attracting a curse. I immediately understood she had been taught the wrong doctrine by someone who does not know how to rightly divide the word into the era in which each verse falls. Her mood changed when I rightly divided the word and gave her the message the Father God had for her within her era, the Grace as it is recorded in Galatians 3:13: *Christ hath redeemed us from the curse of the law, being made a curse for us: for it is written, Cursed is every one that hangeth on a tree.* As soon as she read and understood this, she exclaimed, "Really! Oh wow!" What a relief! Look, you are free from every curse, brothers and sisters! Enjoy the grace! It is called grace for a reason; you didn't do anything to merit it and didn't have to. It is grace indeed.

We earlier mentioned the need to realize when these biblical eras started and when they ended, especially the start of the Grace era and when it would end. It appears to me that the most important division every believer needs to know about and master is the transition from the law to grace. This is where most individuals and even preachers get it all wrong, as reflected in many church rituals that would make you shudder upon realization. When you fully master the art of rightly dividing the word of truth, it would only take a few hours or even minutes of listening to their sermon to tell a church has a glimpse of God. This is because, rightly dividing, will open your eyes to see what God is doing now, in our time.

We've already pointed out that the cross extends into the Gospels. So, when we say the law ended at the cross, it generally implies that most of what we read in Matthew through John applies to those still under the law, except for what's given after the crucifixion. In other words, we need to pay attention to the timeline in these books; what's said before the cross may not be for us, while what's said after the cross is. Although this is true, it may be somewhat misleading if we follow this principle exactly as said, because certain instructions Jesus gave to his disciples before the cross would later form a part of the Christian doctrine. However, when we compare his general message before and after, we will notice a shift and also observe the difference in his response to those not within his fold, whom he gave answers that would apply to the era they lived in. For example, in Luke 10:25-26, a lawyer asked Jesus what he must do to inherit eternal life; Jesus' ultimate response to him was to go and do what is written in the law; in other words, Jesus instructed him to practice the law (Matthew 19: 16-17, Luke 18:19). Jesus has said this because it was before the cross. He knows that the man asking the question is still under the law, and he gives an answer that applies to his era. Jesus gave different instructions as he neared the cross, and this time, to his disciples. He instructed his disciples rather to believe in him in John 14:1, and the same to those who genuinely seek eternal life at other moments (John 3:16-18, John 6:35-40, Luke 8:12). This should also hint us of what to extract and apply when we read the gospels. If you're curious about which books are specifically written for Christians, here's the deal: while the Bible is meant for Christians to read and learn from, the books from Acts to Revelation are directly written for Christians. So, we should also, in this era, read and apply any material in the gospel that does not rely on the law but is endorsed by information found in Acts to Revelation.

The biggest question left unanswered amongst some of those who've been awakened to the true meaning of rightly dividing is the question of the scriptural books of the Old Covenant that do not speak directly to the new creation man. Let's put it this way: We have established that the Bible is written for us, but not everything in it is written to us, and the Apostle

Paul clarified that we are not under the law but under grace. Which Old Testament books are written to us, then? To answer this question, it is best to start by saying that every book with some set of precepts or laws written before the sacrificial death of Jesus is not written to us.

Before we establish this point, let us acknowledge the divisions among theologians. The Old Testament books are divided or classified into the "Law" (Torah), the "Prophets" (Nevi'im), and the "Writings" (Ketuvim). So, it is likely that when we speak of the law, we generally speak of the Torah and Nevi'im when we speak of the book of the prophets. For example, when Jesus said, *"Think not that I am come to destroy the law or the prophets: I am not come to destroy, but to fulfil."* (Matthew 5:17), he referred to the two, Torah and Nevi'im. So, when we say we are not under the law, we refer to Torah. The books Genesis, Exodus, Leviticus, Numbers, and Deuteronomy are included in the Torah, also known as the Pentateuch. Although this may not be a perfect classification because some individuals lived before the law and without the law in Genesis. Genesis should not have been classified as the law for that reason; however, let us proceed without delving much into it. On the other hand, the prophets are books containing both fulfilled, fulfilling, and future unfulfilled events. The fulfilled events will serve as examples unto us (1 Corinthians

10:11), while the fulfilling and the future events are for us to know what to expect.

So, someone may ask, why do we do away with the law since our savior stated categorically that he does not intend to destroy it (Matthew 5:17)? To answer that question, pay close attention to his choice of words, destroy and fulfill, then read the next verse to understand what he is saying in its context. First, we know that he kept the law; if he had violated the laws, that would be tantamount to destroying them. Second, he fulfilled the law (Hebrews 4:15). I have never read of all men who lived before Christ ever described as a man who fulfilled the law save Jesus; they were all said to have kept the law. Making it imperative for Jesus to fulfill the law for the plan of God to progress. The reason is not far-fetched; it is because of the next verse of Matthew 5:17 that we read earlier, which says, *For verily I say unto you, Till heaven and earth pass, one jot or one tittle shall in no wise pass from the law, till all be fulfilled.* Should Jesus destroy these laws as described earlier without fulfilling them, the plan of God, as described in verse 18, would have been distorted. The law must be fulfilled before setting aside, and that is what Jesus meant he intended to do; that is what Matthew 5:17-18 talks about, and that is what Jesus did. The problem is that we have read verse 17 out of context and downplayed the conditional clause, 'till all be fulfilled', for so many years, and each time we approach it, we have our minds preoccupied with the out-of-context reading. When Jesus yelled, "It is finished," on the cross, we learned that what he had finished included fulfilling the law and the prophets, everything written about him. Since all the law is fulfilled, he can sacrifice our Passover from the law to Grace (Hebrews 10:7-9). Therefore, we are under Grace and never under the law anymore. If so, all the instructions, the dos and don'ts in the Torah, the five books, are not written to us. Since the prophets as books consist of fulfilled events and future events, they may not speak to us since we are neither fulfilled nor in the future. Certain prophetic books, however, though fulfilled, contain prophetic messages for our era, those we need to heed. For example, Joel 2:28 speaks of our time, the Generation of the holy spirit. It was seen to be fulfilled first on the day of Pentecost. However, the Holy Spirit has not left us today since after Pentecost, showing that this prophecy of Joel speaks to us and would therefore be classified as a fulfilling event. Therefore, anyone reading the Books of the Prophesies should develop the skill of rightly dividing by knowing whether the prophecy is fulfilled, fulfilling, or for the future.

Lastly, what about the writings (Ketuvim)? Psalms, Proverbs, Job, Song of Solomon, Ruth, Lamentations, Ecclesiastes, Esther, Daniel, Ezra, Nehemiah, and Chronicles comprise the Ketuvim. These books are neither in the law nor the prophets but are called the writings. Most of them, especially Psalms and Proverbs, are wisdom books containing certain timeless information that may be used today. We can always learn from all the Ketuvim. However, one thing we should keep in mind is that even though we can learn from these books, they are not directly written to us. The characters in these books, though known as children of God, are spiritually dead and alienated from God, unlike us in grace, who are spiritually alive and maintain a dear relationship with God. So, lifestyles, laws, and precepts in these books may, therefore, not apply to us who are now spiritually alive and function in the spirit (Romans 8:1B). For example, David in Psalms could speak of humans as his enemies (Psalm 3:7). Still, we won't so speak because the course of battle has changed from the law to grace. Those under the law have human enemies, but in grace, we fight against devils (Ephesians 6:12). Things such as the essence of God, when discussed in the writings, will remain timeless because God's nature never changes (Hebrews 13:8). We must therefore strive to rightly divide as we read the writings (Ketuvim) to only use the information that can apply to us as people under grace.

A great way to approach this is to ask the question, who is this chapter or verse addressing? Then, examine the era in which the recipient lived. If the recipient lived under the law, we may not be among the beneficiaries of any direction or instruction. However, if the recipient is God, it always applies because He exists beyond time. Let us give one practical example. Psalm 23:1:

The Lord is my shepherd; I shall not want.

In this verse, David shares how his sufficiency comes from God. Even though he lived under the old covenant, he speaks of God's provision for His children. Since the focus here is on God, this verse remains relevant to people under grace and the new covenant.

Another key practice is to watch out for certain terminologies that do not apply to Grace and exchange them with what they represent in our era; then, we can apply the information in the writings. For example, the term 'law' must be understood as God's Word or, precisely, doctrines each time we find them in the writings rather than the Mosaic Law or the commandments. So, Psalm 1:2a, for example, *"But his delight is in the law of the Lord,"* We must understand 'delight in the law of the Lord' as 'delight in the word of God' when we read this today and apply it to ourselves.

You might wonder why dividing the Scripture is so crucial that we interpret 2 Timothy 2:15 as an instruction to do so. The reason is simple: first, it's the key to unlocking a true understanding of God's Word. Without it, grasping the meaning of Scripture becomes a challenge. Secondly, it's the only way to ensure you apply biblical truth correctly. You might have heard that learning Greek is essential for truly understanding Scripture, but that's not true.

A practical guide to scriptural clarity

You don't need to know the original manuscript's language—everything you need is already available in your preferred language. The key is to trust what you have and focus on rightly dividing the truth, which unlocks the Word's correct meaning. Let us reiterate that many of the wrong teachings in the churches today come from not knowing how to rightly divide or not paying much-needed attention to it. When people read the scripture and fail to divide rightly, they come up with the statement that "the Bible contradicts itself." There are no such things as contradictory messages in the bible, never! Let us further illustrate the importance of rightly dividing with an example. In Genesis 17:9-14. God instructed Abraham, His child, to keep His covenant by having all male descendants, including household members and servants, circumcised. Circumcision would serve as a sign of this everlasting covenant between God and Abraham's lineage. Every male, starting at eight days old, must undergo this procedure. Those who are not circumcised will be excluded from the community, as they have broken the covenant. Then, in Galatians 5:1-6, the Bible states clearly that circumcision is not important to believers, again, children of God. Someone without the knowledge of rightly dividing would look at these two places in the Bible and run with the notion that they are contrary. What happened is that these are two eras, and God interacts with humans in each of these eras in different ways. We can understand this when we look at the sixth verse of Galatians 5, *For in Jesus Christ neither circumcision availeth anything, nor uncircumcision; but faith which worketh by love.* Remember that when we discussed the term "In Christ Jesus," we implied that it means born again, or Christianity, which we know specifically, in this case, happens in the era of Grace. From this, we have insight into the differences between the periods of the two directives, which account for the differences in the instructions. Galatians 5 was in the grace era, while Abraham's story in Genesis 17 falls under the patriarchal or pre-law era. The examples are countless, but let's take one more. In Exodus 29:38-42, Leviticus 16:3-34, and Numbers 28-29, sacrifices were central to the Israelites' relationship with God, symbolizing atonement, gratitude, and dedication, and God demanded them. But in Hebrews 10:5, the bible says that God does not want the sacrifices. Leviticus was simply under the law, whereas Hebrew was under the grace. Some readers may be surprised at this, especially those who attend churches that still follow practices from times past that don't belong to the current church age. The misconception springs from not rightly dividing the truth, an error on the part of the teaching leadership of the church. Such teachers are not approved by God (2 Timothy 2:15).

Take a moment and reflect on any practices you might be holding onto that don't align with the era of grace. If you find any, now is the perfect time to let them go; God won't recognize you as a faithful student otherwise. The more you journey into the Bible and learn to rightly divide the truth, the more you'll uncover beliefs and habits that do not belong in our time. Don't fight it; don't push back. That's the Holy Spirit urging you to cleanse yourself and walk in the truth.

Some might still argue that "rightly dividing" means understanding the truth from the Bible or separating truth from error. But that's not what the Bible is saying. If that were the case, it would suggest that there are lies or mistakes in Scripture, and there are none. Every word in the Bible is the truth, no matter what era it's from. To summarize, the benefit of rightly dividing is that it allows you to visualize and apply the right instruction at the right time to the right people.

There are sections of the church that understand fully what rightly dividing means, but assign division that seems not to present the truth of God as it should. They present three divisions in the Bible, namely, the time past, now, and the time to come. These divisions draw the idea from Ephesians 2:2-7, where Paul described the time past and now. The idea goes further to group the books of Genesis to Acts into the time past, Romans to Philemon into now, the grace, and Hebrews to Revelation into times to come, and then argue that Christians only need the grace by implication, only Romans to Philemon. This three-division approach seems good and looks promising in understanding and applying the word. But there seems to be a major flaw in the grouping of the scriptures. The problem is that it mistakenly lumps essential teachings of grace with those from other dispensations. Drawing a dividing line from Romans, this method cuts off some foundational Christian truths in books like Acts and John. Take John 15:5, for instance, what Jesus said there still applies to us in this era of Grace. He said, *"I am the vine, ye are the branches: He that abideth in me, and I in him, the same bringeth forth much fruit: for without me ye can do nothing."*

Now the question is, has this changed today? Do we still have to abide? Of course, we do, and that tells us that the Book of John contains certain fundamental doctrines in Christianity, and ignoring these key teachings creates a serious disconnect in understanding the full message of the Gospel.

Unexpectedly, the churches that developed and upheld this three-division concept based many of their rituals on teachings from the Book of Acts. Here's the dilemma: if the Book of Acts supposedly belongs to a past era, why are they incorporating its practices into their liturgy today, in the age of grace? It's a contradiction that raises a serious question about their understanding of scripture and our era. It's evidence of wrongly dividing. Across the other end of the division, drawing a line from Philemon excludes some weighty matters of Christianity and includes them in times to come or future events. A lot of information in the Book of Revelation applies to the Grace era. For example, Revelation 2 and 3 discuss letters written to the seven churches. These churches are in the Grace since the bible did not speak of churches existing in the time to come. As for Hebrews, we can infer if the book is for us from the words of the author at the beginning of the book; let's take a look at Hebrews 1:1: *God, who at sundry times and in divers manners spake in time past unto the fathers by the prophets, hath in these last days spoken unto us by his Son.* We belong on the last day, called Grace. So, there is no way the Book of Hebrews would be grouped into the times to come. That makes this division faulty and capable of distorting our understanding of Scripture.

However, this division method might seem reasonable if we examine it without scrutinizing the specific books within each dispensation, as it blends the pre-law and law eras. Nevertheless, this approach aids application but fails to capture the nuances of divine interaction, which culminates in man's redemption. God's engagement with people under the law was markedly different from how He interacted with them before the law. The positive aspect of the three-division approach is that it promotes a strong foundation in Romans to Philemon, which facilitates being established in the doctrine of grace as outlined in the Pauline epistles. Aside from that, there are clear advantages to adopting this approach or some form of division rather than none.

It may seem that using this three-division method is the best, easiest, and most practical approach to understanding the Bible, especially considering the claim that it was derived from Paul the Apostle's application. At the very least, seeing these terminologies 'in times past,' 'now,' and 'in times to come' used in the Bible itself makes it highly convincing. It is quite easy to be carried away by that without remembering that the Apostle also highlighted the division that acknowledged those who lived before the law. As we've seen in Romans 5:13-14.

To be very clear, Paul does not use the three divisions as the proponents of this method suggest. A strong argument can be made that Paul recognized and utilized five divisions. In Romans 5:13, read above, he states that sin existed before the law, indicating an awareness of the pre-law era. If Paul acknowledged and differentiated between the pre-law and law eras, it is reasonable to conclude that he recognized and applied this distinction in his teachings.

Even though we do not live before the law, the events that occurred before the law are very important to us who live after the law because of the similarity of this era and inferences drawn from the first. For example, Paul the Apostle used an analogy comparing the events before the law to those after it. In Romans 4:3, Paul compares how our righteousness is completely independent of our works to how it was before the law, referencing Abraham, who lived during the pre-law era.

In simple terms, Paul's analogy suggests that Abraham, who lived in the pre-law era, was credited with righteousness solely by believing in God. Likewise, we who live under grace, after the law, are credited with righteousness through faith in Jesus Christ.

Another very important grace era reference drawn from the pre-law era that comes to mind is in Hebrews 7, where Jesus' priesthood was compared with Melchizedek's priesthood. These examples highlight the significance of understanding the pre-law era in understanding our salvation, which is a subject of great importance. In other words, distinguishing between the pre-law and law eras is essential for a clearer understanding of our salvation in the grace era.

Lastly, another widely accepted division provides innocence, conscience, government, patriarchs, law, grace, and the kingdom as the different eras. When we carefully examine this division, we observe that the part we noted as pre-law is split into innocence, conscience, government, and patriarchs. This appears as the best of the division existing until we realize that it does not major in God's interaction with humans. For example, why must we have the conscience, government, and patriarch's eras separated since God's judgment on mankind living in these eras is based on one thing: their conscience? Even though there seems to be no major flaw in this division, it seems filled with superfluous additions.

Before we sign out on this important subject, let us answer another question that may persist in some readers' minds. We believe that Paul was encouraging Timothy to divide the scriptures, and that Jesus was dividing the word of truth during his earth walk. What evidence do we have that assures us that Paul, whom we said gave the advice, was dividing the scripture himself? What about the other early apostles? Did they ever attempt to divide the scripture?

To answer that question, we want to state emphatically that Paul was not just rightly dividing the scripture but also a champion of it. Throughout the epistles of Paul, you will see him dividing the scripture in several places. For example, aside from Romans 5:13, we've seen earlier, Paul severely contrasts the law and grace and often uses the term in Christ to refer to grace. You will also hear him divide the scripture severally using terms such as in times past and now. By the term 'time past,' he mostly refers to either the law or before the law, then uses the term now to refer to Grace. An obvious example is Galatians 3:21-26. Interestingly, Paul spent about five verses discussing our transitioning from the law to grace. Verse 23 is worth memorizing:

But before faith came, we were kept under the law, shut up unto the faith which should afterwards be revealed.

A few important things to point out from this reading. He divided the law from grace and outlined that the law was in fashion before faith, or the grace era, was ushered in. If you had read the sixth verse, you would notice that he argued that justification became possible only in the grace era, but not under the law era, showing how he rightly divided to point out God's dealing with humans in different eras. That is what we would see reading from the end of verse 21 to the beginning of 22, *...verily righteousness should have been by the law. But the scripture hath concluded all under sin....*

One more example of Paul distinguishing between the pre-law era (also referred to as "without the law"), the law, and grace, as previously explained, can also be found in Romans 3:21-22. Let us study this verse carefully; it reads:

But now [in the Grace era] *the righteousness of God without the law* [pre-law era,(example, Abraham, compare it with Genesis 15:6 and Galatians 3:6)] *is manifested, being witnessed by the law and the prophets* [the law era (witnessed in Christ during the earth walk]; *Even the righteousness of God which is by faith of Jesus Christ unto all and upon all them that believe: for there is no difference*:

Feel free to read the analysis repeatedly; you will see how the three connected eras are outlined. Simply put, the righteousness of God endured through these three eras, with similar practices during the pre-law and the grace era.

Concerning the other Apostles, like Peter. Well, they all divided the word of truth, for example, we read his famous vision where God revealed to him that in this new dispensation, that which was considered impure in the old is no more so. We can point out one or two examples of so many other Apostles where they rightly divided the scripture, even though much is not said about their activities.

Why, then, should we read the pre-law, the law, and the future events in the bible? We should read them because they are given to us to read, and when we do, we will see the time-past messages as examples of what we are to practice in the Grace era (1 Corinthians 10:11) and the future events for us to know what to expect. For example, in Exodus 14:13-14, a promise is made to the then-Israelites that can be interpolated to Christians living in the Grace era when they are in distress. Because it is an example of how God cares about and can deliver his people, so, it goes across eras. Secondly, it is about who God is and what He can do, which is timeless. In Numbers 21:4-9, Moses made a bronze serpent and placed it on a pole. Anyone bitten by a snake and looked at the bronze serpent was healed. This is an example of how we are saved from the devil's power when we look to (believe in) Jesus Christ under grace, as explained in John 3:14-15. We can go on and on in showing these examples throughout the scripture. The fundamental thing we must commit to mind is that in grace, we work in the spirit, whereas in times past, we walked in the flesh. Therefore, these examples, when interpolated, would portray spiritual manifestation.

To wrap up, it's important to remember that Jesus Christ ended the old practices and established a new one. Hebrews 10:8-10 is very clear on this: *Above when he said, Sacrifice and offering and burnt offerings and offering for sin thou wouldest not, neither hadst pleasure therein; which are offered by the law; Then said he, Lo, I come to do thy will, O God. He taketh away the first, that he may establish the second. By the which will we are sanctified through the offering of the body of Jesus Christ once for all.* Therefore, we should follow only the commands given in this era of grace.

Let's conclude this chapter by practicing the division methods we've discussed using some Bible passages in a few exercises. Consider Deuteronomy 21:18-21, which specifies capital punishment for stubborn and rebellious children. The passage reads:

18 If a man have a stubborn and rebellious son, which will not obey the voice of his father, or the voice of his mother, and that, when they have chastened him, will not hearken unto them:

19 Then shall his father and his mother lay hold on him, and bring him out unto the elders of his city, and unto the gate of his place;

20 And they shall say unto the elders of his city, This our son is stubborn and rebellious, he will not obey our voice; he is a glutton, and a drunkard.

21 And all the men of his city shall stone him with stones, that he die: so shalt thou put evil away from among you; and all Israel shall hear, and fear.

Now, the question arises: Why is this command not practiced today? The answer is simple: when we rightly divide the Bible, we understand that Deuteronomy falls under the Law, not under Grace. While it was indeed a command from God, it was given for a different time and era. This is how we properly divide Scripture. To reinforce this point, let's look at how the Apostle Paul celebrates the freedom we have in Christ, freedom from the demands of the law, including commands like those in Deuteronomy, writing:

"For the law of the Spirit of life in Christ Jesus hath made me free from the law of sin and death" (Romans 8:2).

Furthermore, recall that we mentioned earlier that when dividing the Wisdom Books, we can learn valuable lessons from them, but their commands may not always apply directly to us today. Let's illustrate this using the example of parents and children discussed earlier. Consider Proverbs 20:20:

"Whoso curseth his father or his mother, his lamp shall be put out in obscure darkness."

This verse in Proverbs aligns with the command in Deuteronomy 21, discussed earlier, and reflects a principle of harsh consequences for dishonoring one's parents, with severe punishment (the "lamp" being extinguished) for such behavior. Under the era of grace, as we've already established, the harsh punitive measures of the Law no longer apply. Instead, parents are encouraged not to exasperate or embitter their children, as seen in Ephesians 6:4 and Colossians 3:21.

Let's consider one more exercise by looking at Revelation 21:1-4:

And I saw a new heaven and a new earth: for the first heaven and the first earth were passed away; and there was no more sea.

2 And I John saw the holy city, new Jerusalem, coming down from God out of heaven, prepared as a bride adorned for her husband.

3 And I heard a great voice out of heaven saying, Behold, the tabernacle of God is with men, and he will dwell with them, and they shall be his people, and God himself shall be with them, and be their God.

4 And God shall wipe away all tears from their eyes; and there shall be no more death, neither sorrow, nor crying, neither shall there be any more pain: for the former things are passed away.

Someone might read the fourth verse and ask, "Why do Christians still experience death, lose loved ones, mourn, go to the hospital, and feel pain when the Bible clearly states that these things will be gone?" We can answer this question using the five division methods. Remember, we stated that many events in Revelation are future events, and reading verse 1 along with verse 4 provides context, showing that these events refer to the future, not the present. Paul, the Apostle, refers to this as the time to come. More examples could lead us further into doctrinal discussions, but for now, the key takeaway is that the reader must continue practicing proper scriptural division as they read Scripture.

It is not unlikely, however, to encounter some folks who will, without knowledge, accuse you of not respecting all the scriptures when you follow the direction laid out in this chapter. So, do not let anyone intimidate you into thinking you are cherry-picking scriptures because that is not what you are doing! You're rightly dividing the Word.

8

GUIDANCE OF THE SPIRIT

Jesus said, *"Howbeit when he, the Spirit of truth, is come, he will guide you into all truth"* (John 16:13). This statement of His refers to the guidance of the holy spirit to which we have devoted this whole chapter. Note that the truth here refers to the word of God, as we also saw in Jesus' prayer in John 17:17: *Sanctify them through thy truth: thy word is truth.* John 16:13 seems to have summed up everything we intend to elaborate on in this chapter. One vital inference we can make from John 16:13 is that the role the holy spirit plays in our attempt to understand the scripture is the role of guidance. To fully understand what this means, let us illustrate it using the lecturing teaching approach in our educational system. There are several roles the holy spirit plays within and outside the believer. But our discussion in this book will be limited to his role in our struggle to understand the Bible, which we have to reiterate looks like a lecturer's role in our educational systems.

Lecturers provide resources for the students and guide them to use the resources to learn. Importantly, the students do the studies themselves while lecturers guide them. Secondly, lecturers are involved in advanced learning, such as the ones done in our colleges and universities. Similarly, the Holy Spirit provides the resources as we have severally established; by saying that our Bible was inspired through him, the Spirit also ensures the Bible is preserved for us. The Holy Spirit guides us while we study the Bible, allowing us to navigate through advanced learning in the Word. We will spend a good amount of our time to understand this concept.

To begin, when we keep reading the scripture, the Holy Spirit's guidance routes our minds to previously learned truth that compares and explains the new information we are learning in most cases. Recall that we have explained how we must compare scripture with scriptures; in most cases, the holy spirits trigger this action. It does not necessarily take a degree in theology to develop the skill of comparing scriptures with scripture, as you may have been told. No, it only takes the indwelling of the holy spirit and your daily effort to read. The Bible is very clear on this:

"Now we have received, not the spirit of the world, but the Spirit who is from God, that we might know the things that have been freely given to us by God. These things we also speak, not in words which man's wisdom teaches but which the Holy Spirit teaches, comparing spiritual things with spiritual" (Corinthians 2:1 to 16 NKJV).

That is why Jesus assures us that when the holy spirit comes, he will guide us into all truth; again, recall the truth is the word, by extension, the bible. We also said that the holy spirit leads us into an advanced understanding of the Word, just as the lecturers guide advanced learners. What do we mean by this? First, let us agree that the lecturing method cannot be used in kindergartens or elementary schools. It is mainly used in higher education, such as colleges and universities, where students are considered advanced learners. We've also said that such a function is like what the holy spirit does in a believer aiming to understand the bible. The Spirit leads the believer's thoughts through a surge of perception, insights, and enlightenment that facilitate advanced learning, what the mere mind cannot conceive: The deep things of God, as we've seen in 1 Corinthians 2:9 to 10:

"But as it is written: "Eye has not seen, nor ear heard, Nor have entered into the heart of man The things which God has prepared for those who love Him." 10 But God has revealed them to us through His Spirit. For the Spirit searches all things, yes, the deep things of God".

These are called the deep things in the sense that they are not on the peripheral or the basic; they are advanced. The natural man - the man without the guidance of the spirit, who reads the scripture with his eyes, ears, and natural mind, cannot grasp these things. The explanation here, in addition to showing us the works of the holy spirit in interpreting the scripture, also helps us settle the argument of whether the scripture could be understood without the Holy Spirit, as some claim. Of course, an unbeliever can read and understand the Scripture; they are written in human language and mostly in the literal sense anyway, but what he is incapable of is understanding the deep things of God. Deep things of God are called revelational knowledge and, sometimes, described as mysteries (Ephesians 3:3-4). Look at Paul the apostle, describing a shift from sense knowledge, the understanding anyone can have, including the unbelievers, to revelational knowledge, which is the deep thing in 2 Corinthians 5:16, he said, *"Wherefore henceforth know we no man after the flesh: yea, though we have known Christ after the flesh, yet now henceforth know we him no more."* Jesus himself in John 3 verse 12 distinguishes the basic and deep things of God in his conversation with Nicodemus, he said: *"If I have told you earthly things, and ye believe not, how shall ye believe, if I tell you of heavenly things?"* Revelational knowledge, which is the advanced learning in Christ or the deep things of God, only comes through the illuminating work of the Holy Spirit.

Someone can ask why these deep things are in the same Bible, but the unbeliever can understand the rest without the deep things. Well, the answer is simple, according to 1 Corinthians 2:11, as a person's thoughts are known only by their own spirit, so the thoughts of God are known only by the Spirit of God, who can reveal them to whomever He chooses—especially those He indwells. The unbeliever can, therefore, understand the basics he needs to know to be saved before he can access the deep things. You can now understand why Jesus again said, *But the Helper, the Holy Spirit, whom the Father will send in My name, He will teach you all things, and bring to your remembrance all things that I said to you* (John 14:26 NKJV). Remember that he said 'all things'; to me, all things include rudimentary and deep things. Are these deep things of God or advanced knowledge necessary? Yes, they are if you desire spiritual growth (Hebrews 5:12 and 6-13).

Having discussed the role of the Holy Spirit in directing our thoughts through comparable scriptures and illuminating our minds with the doctrine of Christ, we'll conclude this chapter by emphasizing that the Holy Spirit knows the thoughts of God, hidden within His Word, and reveals them to those He indwells.

But how does one procure the indwelling of the Holy Spirit? Receiving the Holy Spirit starts with believing in the Lord Jesus Christ. Once you believe, you become saved; once you are saved, God will seal you with the Holy Spirit. To be precise, we can infer from John 2:6-8 and Titus 3:5 that the Holy Spirit born us again as soon as we believe.

What do we mean by 'believe,' which we have mentioned severally? The answer is straightforward: the word is literal; the Bible says, "Believe in the Lord Jesus Christ, and you will be saved" (Acts 16:31). Here's how it works: Believe that Jesus

Christ is the Son of God, who came to Earth to die for your sins (John 3:16). Recognize that your good deeds or behavior can't save you or make you right with God, but only Jesus' sacrifice on the cross can.

You still have the chance if you haven't made this decision yet. It only takes a moment. A simple prayer expressing your decision to believe won't hurt; it's simple, and that's all it might take. Look at what the bible says:

If thou shalt confess with thy mouth the Lord Jesus, and shalt believe in thine heart that God hath raised him from the dead, thou shalt be saved (Romans 10:9).

9

STARTING YOUR BIBLICAL JOURNEY

"What is the best order to read the Bible?" is one of the most frequently asked questions by people who plan to journey through the Bible. At times, both new and seasoned believers ask these questions mainly to unravel the most effective order to read the Bible for better understanding and clarity. I have encountered countless believers wondering where to start, how to proceed, where to read more, what to major in, and where to read less. Some others would ask, does reading order matter? As much as we will try to answer all these questions in this chapter. It seems that the best question should have been, "Does the Bible provide any specific order to be followed in reading its books?" for easy understanding and comprehension.

The answer to the very last question is no. There seems to be no Bible-based laid-out order to follow in the study of the Bible; most of the suggestions in this chapter, therefore, are not set in stone. Many ideas would be suggested based on what worked for several people, and perhaps me. We know that one of the ways to attain greatness in practice is to step into the footprints of the giants, and this principle underscores some of the ideas laid out in this chapter. Since the ideas have worked for others, they might be useful if carefully followed. Nevertheless, some bible-backed ideas and practices that would ease understanding of the bible and help build up doctrine, aside from reading order, would also be shared in this chapter, which must be heeded.

In terms of where to start, it is recommended to start with the New Testament, then move on to the Old Testament, and return to the New Testament after completing the entire Bible. It's particularly helpful to start with the Gospel of John when beginning the New Testament, as it is often viewed as more theological and easier for new readers to grasp. After John, continue with Matthew, Mark, and Luke, then proceed through the rest of the New Testament, following the order from Acts to Revelation. When reading the Old Testament, it can be helpful to follow the order in which the books are arranged, starting with Genesis and ending with Malachi.

Some Bible books deserve more time and attention, especially considering how much we can take away from them. So those books, we must revisit after completing the entire Bible, and spend extra time on them. Proverbs and Psalms are books that deserve more attention and extra time in the Old Testament. In the New Testament, Paul's epistles are the books you must devote your time to. Acts and the Gospel of John also deserve similar attention and time as you gave to Proverbs and Psalms. But, of course, dwell on the epistles of Paul.

A practical guide to scriptural clarity

You might be wondering why these reading suggestions were made. Let's explore the reasoning behind them. Beginning the journey with the book of John helps introduce you to the mission of Jesus Christ on earth. It clarifies the concept of eternal life and offers the opportunity to believe and be saved, paving the way for understanding and utilizing the role of the Holy Spirit (John 3:16). If you skip the chapter on the Spirit's role, it's worth pausing to go back and read it. The Gospels - Matthew, Mark, Luke, and John- provide a detailed account of Jesus' life, teachings, death, and resurrection, presenting the message from different perspectives. Reading the rest of the New Testament will guide you into Christianity and help you understand the essence of the Christian journey.

Reading the Old Testament from Genesis will allow you to study the creation, the fall, and God's early interaction with mankind. Apart from that, reading Genesis to Malachi will present the Bible to you as a message rather than as a mystery book. You will start to realize how we got here, our trajectory to the recent day Christian practices. You will also understand God's redemption plan from day one of the fall. You will see Jesus walking behind the scenes in the Old Covenant, then on the center stage in the New Covenant. One thing that will stand out to you is that the Old Testament will become a mirror image of the New Testament as you proceed (1 Corinthians 10:11). Spending more time on the epistles of Paul, especially the book of Romans, will provide a thorough explanation of Christian doctrine. Paul's epistles will ground the reader in the faith. Psalms and Proverbs in the Old Testament are wisdom books that provide encouragement and principles applicable to daily life. This method of study allows the reader to travel through the bible and ensure they touch every burning issue throughout the bible. Other than journeying through the bible, it is important to mention that each book can be revisited at any time, as needed.

Another effective study style, different from the journey-type approach described above, is the topical studies approach, where the reader explores the scripture based on specific themes. This method works best if you have a solid understanding of Christ's doctrine. The reader can delve deeply into various subjects and spend time analyzing cross-references and the usage of terminology throughout the Bible. The study approach enables you to compare scripture with scripture and promotes spiritual growth. The topical approach also makes it easier to discuss the subjects being reviewed with others. Many preachers use this study method to prepare their sermons; we must stress that the study style is not reserved for them. Any devoted believer can always choose a subject and research it. When a believer encounters an unfamiliar concept when reading the Bible, he must take time to thoroughly investigate it. For example, let's say the student ran into baptism. The student can research this idea by examining all the biblical perspectives around it, including its meaning, implications, and genesis, among other things. Since this is how a believer can question even the teachings they encounter, I think no sincere believer should shun this Bible study method as they mature in grace. Topical bible study methods could accomplish or explore much more than theological interrogations and sermon construction. But the utmost advice regarding this style is to allow the Holy Spirit to lead you in this exploration.

People approach topical studies of the Bible in various ways, and we cannot determine with certainty which of these approaches is correct or incorrect. One method is to begin with a certain keyword and look up every Bible passage containing the examined terms. People who use the Software Bibles, which are made feasible by technological advances, frequently do this. Another efficient and effective approach is to start with a keyword encountered during reading. For instance, when the reader encounters the phrase "born again" in John 3:3, and desire to explore its meaning. Should the reader misinterpret the term "rebirth" as reincarnation, as advocated by certain religions, this would be a misunderstanding, as it conflicts with other portions and the overall message of the Bible and violates the rules of biblical interpretation. The student is faced with the option of using the most effective approach, which is to use other Bible verses to define the term in its proper context and uncover its meaning, as we've seen in previous chapters. In this case, comparing John 3:3 with 1 John 5:1 can reveal that believing in Jesus Christ is what it means to be born again. This study could then progress by examining 1 Peter 1:23, which explains that being born again happens through the word of God, and 1 John 3:9, which highlights how being born again addresses the issue of sin in the believer's life. Through this process, the reader can develop a well-rounded understanding and build a sound doctrine by thoroughly exploring the topic. As previously mentioned, one valuable advantage of topical studies is their ability to help readers critically assess the sermons they hear. For instance, if a sermon suggests that good deeds are required to be born again, the reader's study above would equip them to recognize such a claim as inconsistent with biblical teachings and confidently reject it.

Now, let us address whether having a study plan is truly necessary, which is a significant consideration, especially with the abundance of Bible study plans available today, including the popular one-year plans that promise to guide readers through the entire Bible in just twelve months. The best way to answer this question is to look at the pros and cons of following a study plan, although its success largely depends on the individual. The primary benefit of using these study plans is accountability. These plans are structured to ensure the reader covers the Bible within a specific timeframe. Additionally, yearly study plans promote commitment by outlining daily readings for the user. They are also thought to enhance understanding of the Bible, being designed to help readers grasp the context more effectively. However, the rigid structure of these plans can be problematic for some readers. The lack of flexibility of these study plans leaves little room for personalized exploration of the Bible. This rigidity may hinder some individuals from fully enjoying their readings or experiencing genuine spiritual growth. Another significant concern is the pressure these plans can place on readers. The daily reading schedule can feel overwhelming, particularly for busy people, potentially leading to burnout or skipped readings. As a result, some readers may prioritize completing the readings quickly over truly understanding and reflecting on the content.

Notwithstanding, some individuals can incorporate a few minutes of topical study or bible theme explorations and complete their daily readings when following these yearly plans. Therefore, the necessity of the yearly plan lies in the reader's flexibility, speed, and skill level. The Bible student can also make a plan of his own based on his daily schedule and skill level. Individual scheduling one's bible study plan should not undermine the importance of studying the bible daily. That said, creating a plan that excites and energizes the reader rather than leaving them feeling drained or overwhelmed is important. Whether creating a personalized study plan or using a pre-structured yearly plan, the key is to avoid undue pressure. The explanation given so far implies that choosing a plan, either a purchased annual plan or a self-designed plan, is up to the student to decide. If you thrive on challenges and enjoy pushing yourself to accomplish tasks, a purchased yearly plan might be perfect for you. If otherwise, a flexible reading plan with room for breathing space might be just what you need. The key is consistency; no matter what, ensure you're reading the Bible daily (Psalm 1:2 & Joshua 1:8). Your reading plan doesn't need to be confined to just one year but should be steady, ongoing, and fun.

The most enjoyable, flexible, and fulfilling approach is to ensure you gain at least one message from the Bible each day. This could be from a single verse or an entire chapter; what matters is that you hear something meaningful. Don't get too comfortable going to bed at night without first asking yourself, "What has my Heavenly Father spoken to me about today?" Consider reading a full chapter each day for a bit more of a challenge. This approach lets you aim to complete the Bible quickly while still keeping things comfortable. If something doesn't quite click on your first read, don't hesitate to review it or take a few moments of topical studies. Re-reading can reveal insights you might have missed the first time, while topical studies clarify concepts or terms. Some chapters are longer than others, but sticking to a simple plan of one chapter a day gives you room to breathe; no pressure, just freedom to enjoy and reflect on what you've read. With 1,189 chapters across the 66 books of the Bible, completing one chapter each

A practical guide to scriptural clarity

day means you'd finish the Bible in 1,189 days, roughly 39 months, or just over 3 years. This steady pace leaves plenty of space for deeper meditation without feeling rushed. Again, it is up to you to make plans that may work best for you according to your reading speed, attention capacity, tenacity, strength, and comprehension ability.

To enhance your reading experience and deepen your comprehension, utilize a few pivotal practices, which include embracing daily Bible reading, beginning each session with prayer, utilizing a study Bible for greater insight, reflecting thoughtfully on what you read, engaging with a Bible study group for communal growth, and, most importantly, acting on the word. These steps will help transform your understanding and enrich your spiritual journey.

Dedicating time each day to read the Bible is more than just a good habit; it's a powerful strategy for deepening your understanding. As Joshua 1:8 tells us, daily engagement with Scripture can lead to prosperity and success. By embracing this wisdom, we set ourselves on a path to grasp the word of truth and enrich our lives. Daily Bible reading will make you more adept with words and significantly boost your comprehension skills. Secondly, an everyday Bible reading routine opens a treasure trove of messages and insights. This daily practice equips you with the wisdom needed to weave Scripture together, allowing you to compare and connect verses easily, the act we described earlier as comparing scripture with scripture. Daily reading ignites a deeper passion and fervor for the Word of God, fueling your love, desire, and enthusiasm. Show me a believer who delights in the Lord, and I will show you one who studies the Word frequently. The delightedness eliminates the mental fatigue that distorts attention and understanding.

Praying before reading the bible is another important practice to enhance attention and ensure we consume the right information. If we pray before we resume work, pray before we eat, and before we embark on a journey, what stops us from doing the same when studying the Word? One of the benefits of praying before the reading is to invite the guidance of the Holy Spirit, as we have seen before. The Holy Spirit is the perfect communicator and can guide you through the book he inspired. Today, we say experience is the best teacher, but not with the Word of God; the Holy Spirit is the best teacher for the Word of God. Another benefit of praying is to shut the doors of distractions. The adversary can raise an imaginary storm or inspire an unwarranted visit just to derail your plan of diligence to the word. A simple prayer can avert all or any of that. Remember that our prayers' content can vary depending on our height in grace. Pray as you are led. But if you are not yet a believer, the very first prayer, and perhaps the only one you need to offer, is a heartfelt confession of your belief in Christ, just as the Bible instructs,

A practical guide to scriptural clarity

"That if thou shalt confess with thy mouth the Lord Jesus, and shalt believe in thine heart that God hath raised him from the dead, thou shalt be saved" (Romans 10:9).

Using a study bible is another vital practice to help your understanding of the Bible. We have repeatedly said that we must compare scripture with scripture; the study bible comes in handy because it provides the resources to aid this act. It is probably the most profound benefit of using a study bible. On each, certain verses are italicized alphabets, which provide links to other bible portions that could explain the verse with the italicized alphabets. These explanatory verses are often found between the double lines in the middle of the study bible. So, to compare a verse you read, look up the linked book, chapter, and verse in the middle of the double lines as depicted by the alphabet in what you read. In addition, some study Bibles could give cultural and historical context to help the reader understand difficult passages and big theological ideas. However, be warned that the extra notes or the so-called footnotes in certain Bibles cannot equate with the authority of the inspired word.

Meditating on the word can impact our understanding of the Bible. We know that meditation on God's word benefits the believer in numerous ways. But we are limiting our benefits discussion to the ability to understand the bible. First and foremost, taking the time to meditate on what you read helps solidify those ideas in your mind. Similarly, when you meditate on the word, you retain the word (Colossians 3:16). Then the retained words of God become instantly accessible for comparing Scriptures and for putting into practice. Not only that, recall that we've talked about the instruction to Joshua, from which we inferred that immersing ourselves in the Word day and night opens the door to true success (Joshua 1:8), and we argued that we could also be successful in our understanding of the Word. The instruction to meditate day and night essentially means to reflect and immerse ourselves constantly or frequently. This approach is not just theoretical; it's practical. The more you mull over something, the clearer it becomes, unveiling insights with each reflection. Do you know that Colossians 3:16 will only become a reality when you meditate on the word of God?

Joining a Bible Study Group is another practice that may improve our chances of understanding the scriptures; it is almost self-explanatory, as they say iron sharpens iron. A bible study group will enable you to share ideas, ask questions, get clarification, build doctrines, and foster a better understanding. The benefit of being part of a group is like the effect we get from attending school, where we go to get taught. This is a spot the local church should occupy in the life of an enthusiastic believer. You are responsible for finding a local congregation that can play this role. Churches that maintain their Biblical place are not too numerous without demeaning the body of Christ. Yet it is your responsibility as a believer to search & discern using the resources in the bible (1 John 4:1).

Lastly, acting on the word is presumably the most important. It was initially difficult for me to convince myself that putting the Word of God into practice can help our understanding of the Word. You might be troubled by that uncertainty as you come to this point, but do you know that the application reinforces learning? When we put biblical teachings into practice, we move beyond theoretical knowledge to practical experience. This application helps solidify our understanding of the principles and truths in Scripture. Studying and acting on the word also leads to the renewal of our minds (Romans 12:2) and aligns our thoughts and perspectives more closely with the scriptural doctrines. Remember that these doctrines are what we pick each time we study.

In addition to what is said above, do you know that we grow spiritually as we live out God's word? This growth often brings deeper insights into the meanings and implications of biblical messages, the insights we described earlier as mysteries of the word or deep things in Christ. We saw it in 1 Corinthians 2:14: *But the natural man receiveth not the things of the Spirit of God: for they are foolishness unto him: neither can he know them, because they are spiritually discerned.* Remember that the unbeliever is the natural man described here; he had neither encountered Christ nor had any spiritual growth. I remember when I attempted to evangelize a friend, he said, "What is it that you Christians believe? That someone died for me?" Is that not crazy?" he said. This guy could not get it. He continued, "I didn't do anything wrong, so no one should die for me." Immediately, he looked at me and asked me if that was not crazy; I did not succumb to shame and stagger away from the confrontation because I had already acted on the word that says 'believe!'. So, I am convinced that someone died for me, and I am also convinced that there was a need for him to die for me; I hope you are! Do you know what rather came to my mind at that moment of confrontation? It was 1 Corinthians 1:18, *For the preaching of the cross is to them that perish foolishness; but unto us which are saved it is the power of God.* Those words strengthened me again because I have believed the Gospel, that is, I have acted on the word of God that says Believe the Gospel.

Another straightforward example to illustrate this is acting on the word that says, 'go ye into the world and preach.' It places us in the position to teach the word, and we know that teaching through discussions and reflections enhances learning. Countless examples reveal how living out the Word can profoundly expand your understanding of Scripture. Let these few illustrations inspire you to embody the teachings of the Bible. Our submission thus far in a few of the preceding paragraphs agrees with the Holy Spirit's encouragement through the pen of Brother James, which reads:

"But be ye doers of the word, and not hearers only, deceiving your own selves." (James 1:22).

James 1:22 not only encourages us to act on the word but also describes the act of reading Scripture without applying it as self-deception. If so, it implies that a person who studies Scripture without living by it is not only hindering their own spiritual growth but also will not become a better student of the Word, meaning, they will never attain scriptural clarity nor experience the benefits that come from practicing what the Scriptures teach. If you seek a richer, more nuanced grasp of its messages, immersing yourself in its practice, act on the word, for therein lies the key to unlocking its full depth.

10

PITFALLS TO AVOID

Most interpretations of the bible that miss the mark are not done on purpose; some are honest blunders caused by stumbling into certain traps on the path of understanding the thoughts of God. Pitfalls in our context refer to these traps, which are distractors significant enough to detour our attention from God's intended messages in the Bible. Most of these are visible enough that we observe them without much effort; others are so subtle that we will consider them as either normal or insignificant. If we must understand the mind of God from the scripture, we must avoid these distractors that may end up being roadblocks.

Relying on the traditional understanding or conventional ideas is certainly the biggest of the pitfalls to watch out for. Traditional interpretations have been given to the bible, or certain orthodox Christian doctrines, that have existed for ages. We often do not care if these doctrines spring from the bible but believe and retain them without question, hook, line, and sinker, just because they make sense to us. For example, we have been told that once we sin, such as telling a lie, fighting, and so on, we've been booked for hell. We have not made any effort to read the bible for ourselves to see if what

A practical guide to scriptural clarity

we have been told from birth is what is written in the Bible. But what if you read the Bible and see for yourself that it is not your sin of lying or fighting that would take you to hell? How easy would that be for you to take home? Rather, what we have found ourselves doing is to question what we read when it contradicts the conventional ideas, or assume that it must be saying something else, or that it has other spiritual meanings. We then juggle bible verses, often taken out of context, and quotes from several sources to make sure we suppress the new information we found in the Bible in favor of conventional ideas. We found ourselves doing so because these new ideas contradict the traditional and passed-down doctrines that may have no scriptural bearing. A glaring example is to question why a good man would go to the lake of fire just because he refused to believe in Christ Jesus, as we read from the bible. We see this often because we have been told that we must keep good behavior to make heaven or escape hell. But certainly, this is not what the Bible teaches.

These traditionalists with the bible in their hands will bring your attention to all other religions of the world and their positions on morality. It is quite unfortunate because Christianity is not even a religion like each of those they compare with, underlining the reason you must read the bible for yourself for a personal encounter with the Lord Jesus. In case you are already asking yourself if what you are reading from this book is indeed what the bible says, let us take some readings together, and ensure to put all the how-to study we have discussed so far in this book into practice. John 14:6, *Jesus saith unto him, I am the way, the truth, and the life: no man cometh unto the Father, but by me.* John 3:18 *He that believeth on him is not condemned: but he that believeth not is condemned already, because he hath not believed in the name of the only begotten Son of God.* These two examples make it clear: according to the Bible, even a good person who refuses to believe in the Son of God will face the lake of fire. So why do we hesitate to this single message when we read passages like this? It's often because tradition has taught us differently. Here is a beautiful suggestion therefore when encountering new teachings that challenge your previous knowledge, ask yourself, "What two Bible verses can support these?" Among the two challenging pieces of information you are contrasting, one will always align with several or at least one other portion of the scripture, while the other won't. This approach helps us navigate truth versus tradition.

Another trap we must avoid is reading the Bible with preconceived opinions. This often happens when we hold onto traditional, personal, or learned views. The right approach is to first study the Scripture with an open mind to understand the context, the idea, and the message before comparing it to other previously learned verses to build doctrines. For example, we encountered the word heart in earlier chapters,

A practical guide to scriptural clarity

in our review of Psalm 73:1, where it was used in the context of a 'pure heart.' Now, imagine someone reading the Bible with the preconceived notion that heart only refers to the physical organ in the chest. They might interpret 'pure heart' as simply being free of heart disease, which is not the meaning intended in Scripture. Our example may seem obvious, but it's quite easy to slip into this trap when you look up all Bible verses that mention or use a word or phrase. Sometimes, readers assume that a word or phrase will have the same meaning in every verse where they are found. However, just like in English, the meaning of a word can change depending on the context. Linguistic scholars would agree with me that a word's meaning is shaped by how and where it's used, which is no different in the Bible. For example, take the two sentences: "My hands are clean" and "I clean my hands." Both use the word "clean," but in different ways. Clean in one of the phrases is an adjective meaning innocent, and the other is a verb meaning to wash. Take the word heart again, for example, it is used many times throughout the Bible, often with different meanings depending on the context. In the Psalms, it frequently refers to the innermost being or spirit of a person, as seen in Psalm 51:10. In contrast, in John 14:1, heart refers more specifically to emotions, such as fear or anxiety. Looking up all the instances of a word in the Bible isn't a bad practice, but don't assume the word in review means the same thing every time and everywhere it appears.

Here is another wonderful suggestion to help avoid this: allow the context of the portion read to guide you, not any preconceived ideas.

Appealing to authority is the next pitfall we must avoid. This is a well-known logical fallacy known as 'argumentum ad verecundiam,' which means appeal to authority. We can break this down as exalting the opinions of authorities over what we have seen to be the truth, which is what we are reading ourselves from the scripture. For example, imagine reading in Hebrews 2:14 that Satan holds the power of death, while your trusted pastor tells you that only God can take life because He is the giver of life. You might believe your pastor's opinion, thinking the verse you read must mean something else. This is a common scenario where appealing to authority can derail your understanding of Scripture. Many people think an argument is true just because an authority figure or expert says so, without looking for evidence or reasoning. This kind of thinking is quite common nowadays. Church members so esteem their church leaders that every word from their lips is more revered than anyone can read in the bible. Those people get very uncomfortable when someone questions what their pastors or church leaders say. They believe their word is final, even when the Bible does not support it.

The same could be said for individuals with the know-it-all mindset. By that, we mean individuals who think their understanding of a subject is unquestionable. Know-it-all mindsets could hinder correction, feedback, and redirection when needed. Understanding the Bible requires thoughtful reasoning. Just because someone has a better grasp than another doesn't mean they're always right. Therefore, placing them in that position would elevate them to the role of the Holy Spirit, which is dangerous. It's amusing how people with a "know-it-all" attitude react when you challenge them with Scripture. They might accuse you of lacking the Holy Spirit or claim you read the Bible like any other book. Don't let anyone belittle you! We will all stand before the judgment seat of Christ, no matter our status. If the mighty will stand just as the little, then no one has absolute authority over God's Word. That does not mean we might not be wrong or misunderstand what we read at times. That is why we have to reason the word of God; the one with a better grasp would present a better argument using the Bible to put us right.

Another pitfall to avoid is letting our worldview overshadow the teachings of the Bible. Our worldview could come from culture or tradition, and cultural influence can be a major obstacle in interpreting Scripture. When we impose our cultural perspective on the Bible, it can distort the meaning of the message. For example, "sacrifice" means different things in different cultures. In the East and African cultures, it might be seen as a ritual offering to a deity, while in the West, it's often understood as giving up something important. If cultural context is necessary, we should consider the culture of the original recipients, often the East. Beyond culture, worldviews shaped by traditions, proverbs, science, politics, law, media, philosophy, peers and community, or family and upbringing can also conflict with the Word of God. A beautiful suggestion, once more, is to avoid using these views to define the words you read from the scripture, except when other portions buttress the description.

Ignoring language dynamics is another challenging roadblock we may face on our way to understanding the Bible. The English language has changed over time. Certain terms that had certain meanings when the Bible was written might not have the same connotations in today's culture. Ignoring these changes could cause one to miss the correct message conveyed by the evolving words used in the Bible's translation. Let's illustrate these shifts with a few changed terms in our generation. In the 20th century, the word "hot" might have meant "capable of burning," but in the 21st century, it signifies "extremely pleasant." In terms of the Bible, the term "Holy Ghost" is a prime example, or more specifically, Ghost, as we have already briefly discussed. The King James version of the Bible uses the word Holy Ghost, or more specifically, Ghost, interchangeably with the more modern word Spirit. Here is a precise example. The term "workout" in the Bible translators' clause "work out your salvation" in Philippians 2:12 has evolved. Its meaning has since evolved and been ingrained in our daily lives to mean exercise. Since the word "workout" now means "exercise," someone who doesn't understand language dynamics would easily take it as meaning "exercise your salvation," which is never what was intended. To fully understand its lessons, we must match our understanding of the Bible's words with their meanings at the time of translation. This endeavor guarantees that the timeless truths of scripture are correctly comprehended in their original depth and clarity.

Overemphasizing the Bible's original languages is a trap we may need to avoid, and it's the final pitfall we'll explore in this book. Many preachers habitually dig into the original Bible languages, and when they do, they change the English words in the version they read. But is it worth going down the rabbit hole of looking up the Greek and Aramaic words, especially if you have to tweak the English translation of those words? For example, I listened to a preacher trying to interpret 2 Timothy 2:15. He first investigated the Greek word translated as 'study,' then changed it to 'diligence,' and used diligence to twist the message the way it pleases him. In a way, it seems like constantly referring to the original languages suggests a lack of trust in the expertise of the translators of the English Bible. Secondly, it also suggests a lack of trust in God's ability to preserve His word as promised. If we believe that God has preserved His words, we must trust this preservation to extend to the words used in the English translation, ensuring His message remains unadulterated. Again, if we constantly turn to the original languages to reinterpret the Bible whenever we're uncomfortable with the message, it suggests we doubt that God has truly preserved His Word. In that case, how is this approach different from the modern paraphrased translations we criticized earlier? This approach just means we're twisting the Bible's words to fit messages we're comfortable with, which might not reflect God's true intent. Instead, we must learn to read and rely on the English rendering of the chosen versions, preferably the King James.

Many of the folks who found themselves often changing the words used in the popular bible versions key into the notion that no English version of the bible is a perfect translation. They argue that only the original languages are inspired, not the translations, which could be prone to human error since they weren't created under the direct inspiration of the Holy Spirit. Fortunately, the Holy Spirit, who inspired the Bible, didn't stop working during the translation period and resumed in our time. If God truly kept His promise to preserve His Word, then there must be an infallible English version, with the Holy Spirit fully involved in its translation. King James Version, which is based on Textus Receptus, demonstrates a high degree of infallibility compared to other translations. After examining the histories behind the manuscripts used for various Bible versions, it seems that Textus Receptus stands out as the most reliable, unlike the critical texts.

A practical guide to scriptural clarity

Furthermore, the Bible's original text was carefully written with specific words to convey particular meanings and messages. We spent time discussing how great care was taken in the earlier chapters while documenting and copying the scriptural books. If such measures, such as frequent washing of hands before and after writing the words and keeping dedicated pens for some words, were applied, how much more is the care taken to ensure the precise choice of words used in the translations? Changing these words can alter the intended message.

In conclusion, delving into Greek words to reinterpret their English meanings can be seen as us telling God what He should have said. The God who promised to preserve His Word also chose the English words used in the translations to fulfill that promise. If we believe that no Bible version is accurate as it stands and try to alter the words, we are essentially accusing God of not keeping His promise to preserve His Word.

11

A PRACTICAL GUIDE

Let's sum it all up! Let's bring everything that we've talked about in this book to a summary. This chapter aims to present the major themes discussed so far in a clear, step-by-step format. It is designed for readers who may not have the time or inclination to read an entire book, especially a lengthy one. It concisely summarizes the instructions and insights found throughout this text. It is important to emphasize reading the entire book to fully grasp the details of each suggestion outlined in the practical guide. This chapter is also intended to serve as a practical reference. Readers or Bible students can consult this section while studying the Bible or keep it alongside them to follow its directions until the described approach is fully mastered.

To begin with, we have demonstrated that to understand the bible, we must procure the right Bible Version. To that effect, we have recommended the King James Version (KJV), which is predominantly used in this text. We have also suggested getting the New King James Version (NKJV) for those who want the bible written in our modern English and those who find it extremely difficult to understand the archaic words used in the KJV. The reader is free to use any version they believe to be infallible, aside from the above recommendations.

Second, rather than just reading the Bible, we must study it. Studying the Bible should be approached using the same methods as studying school texts. We must recognize the distinction between reading and studying; reading is the act of reading books for pleasure or to get information, whereas studying entails actively interacting with the material to acquire knowledge and mastery. To grasp the proper meaning, we must read the words as they occur in the text without paraphrasing them and pay attention to commas, full stops, semicolons, and other punctuation. Any study techniques we use in school to ace our exams can be applied to studying the scripture, including questioning, analysis, synthesis, problem-solving, and reflection.

Third, remember that the Bible should be taken literally unless the literal interpretation is illogical. It is intended to be comprehended as humans speak to one another because it is written in human language. We should also be aware that, unless there is a compelling reason to the contrary, we should take statements at face value when we read them. The words of the Bible are figurative when their literal interpretation is illogical, and we should identify the figure of speech employed. For example, when we read statements like

"And he shall be like a tree planted by the rivers of water, that bringeth forth his fruit in his season; his leaf also shall not wither; and whatsoever he doeth shall prosper" (Psalm 1:3),

we should understand that the figure of speech used here is similar because it could not be taken literally. In other words, the literal rendering that suggests humans bear fruit is illogical at face value. Similarly, when we read statements like *Let the floods clap their hands: let the hills be joyful together* (Psalm 98:8), we must see it as a metaphor that cannot be logical either.

Fourth, we must follow Bible interpretation rules if we must understand the bible correctly. Rule number one is to let the scripture interpret the Scripture. By this, we mean that we must compare a reading from the scripture with another portion of the scripture to understand the message. The feasibility of this practice is a function of the amount of the word of God that is retained in our souls. When we act on the word of God in Colossians 3:16, we facilitate and make comparing scripture with scripture seamless. This we will accomplish by reading the bible daily, retaining what we read, and acting on what we read.

Rule of bible interpretation number two is that no scripture must be interpreted in isolation. This looks like the first rule we discussed, but it is different. It simply says that any idea found in one portion of the bible would not make a doctrine

A practical guide to scriptural clarity

or a point unless another portion buttresses that point or says the same thing. This rule also expects us to study and retain the words to reproduce and match them with any newly learned items. The rule operates on the premise that each bible account is a testimony of its author, and testimonies of more than one must establish every word, as we've found in 2 Corinthians 13:1. This rule also emphasizes that every message we derive from our reading must align with the overall context of the Bible's teachings. Therefore, no interpretation of a single verse should contradict another verse or the Bible's entire message.

Rule number three is to read and understand bible messages in context. This rule sounds self-explanatory, but it is important to understand and apply while reading the scripture. The context is more like the background of a text, and we know the place it holds in understanding English conversations. It is also important to understand that the context could be at a phrase, sentence, verse, chapter, or whole book level. In most cases, we can understand the context if we ask why this is written, who it addresses, and on what occasion it was written. For example, a word can mean several things based on the passage's context. A wonderful illustration from the Bible is the word "world." The term in John 3:16, "For God so loved the world," refers to all humanity. But in 1 John 2:15, "Do not love the world or the things in the world," the same term "world" refers to the devil and his devil-inspired practices.

Rule number four is to be loud where the Bible is loud and be silent where the Bible is silent. In other words, stick to what the Bible says and avoid speculating on what it doesn't. This means that when reading Scripture, don't make assumptions. If it's not written, it didn't happen, and just because something doesn't make sense to you doesn't mean the Bible is wrong with that. Also, avoid approaching the Bible with preconceived ideas, whether they come from stories we've heard growing up or traditions passed down by our ancestors. One of the most obvious ways people fail this rule is by giving explanations the bible did not give.

Rule number five is not to interpret the bible with experience, but rather to explain experience with the bible. Please do not conclude that some things are not the true meaning of the documented accounts, because it seems impossible with experience. However, the scripture can explain the experiences, including the reason behind the impossibility.

The fifth step to understanding the bible is to nurture certain crucial habits when it comes to studying our Bible, and that is the act of rightly dividing it. We must establish that rightly dividing the word of truth, as stated in 2 Timothy 2:15, is the most important aspect of Bible interpretation. The Scriptures assure us that the word "divide" is the actual practice intended for a Bible student in the instruction in 2 Timothy 2:15, because other words, such as "expounding," existed at the time of the epistle's writing. Yet, the author chose the word "divide." He was not being fanciful because he was not writing fiction; he chose the right word, "divide," because that is what the Holy Spirit wants us to do.

The Bible, which we know as the word of truth, must be understood as containing the New and Old Testaments, which are an obvious division. But the most important division we must actively make to understand the Bible rightly includes dividing the Bible into the periods: Before the Law, the Law, the Grace, the Tribulation, and the Millennial Reign. The distinction between these eras is important because God deals with people differently in each era. We need to understand that we are under the period of grace and, therefore, will practice the instructions given within the era of grace. Furthermore, we cannot go back and pick the instructions given under the Law to obey them because that would not be consistent with God's dealing with us in this era, since God does not deal with us today the way He dealt with people in previous dispensations. At the same time, we cannot utilize advice meant for a future era, as that would also be inconsistent with God's timely dealing with individuals. It is important to understand when each era begins and ends. The era of grace began at the death of Christ Jesus and will end when Jesus takes us home (called the rapture). Some may argue that grace started on the day of Pentecost when the Holy Spirit was poured out. I will leave you to study your Bible and decide.

One of the key takeaways from this book is understanding how to correctly apply the Bible in today's world, which is the main idea behind rightly dividing the Word. We should follow every instruction from the books of Acts to Jude unless they refer to future events. We can also look for relevant guidance in the book of Revelation and the four gospels (Matthew to John) that apply to the era of grace. However, the instructions from the Law are not meant for us to follow, no matter how moral they seem. Psalms and Proverbs, while full of wisdom and life lessons, should be seen as guides for strategy rather than strict commands.

Remembering that our battles are now spiritual, not physical, since we've moved from the Law to Grace, is crucial. So, when we read about enemies, we should think about spiritual opposition, like the devil, not people. To determine if a passage applies to us, it's best to compare it with teachings from the grace period, especially Paul's epistles.

The sixth is a fundamental principle we must adopt when reading the Bible; it is to neither add nor take away from its words. This addition can be done intentionally or unintentionally to win arguments or prove a point. However, once a word is added, no matter how pleasant, powerful, or inspiring it may seem, it is no longer God's Word. Additions can also occur when we read with preconceived notions, usually influenced by tradition. On the other hand, subtraction happens when we overlook or ignore certain words or downplay their presence in a sentence. We emphasize that every word of Scripture is inspired and should be given proper attention. In other words, no word in the Bible is insignificant.

Seventh, we must acknowledge the role of the Holy Spirit in understanding Scripture. The Holy Spirit plays the role of a lecturer, guiding us to gain more advanced knowledge of the Bible, also known as the deep things of God or revelational Knowledge. While an unbeliever, without the indwelling of the Holy Spirit, can read and grasp the basic messages of Scripture, since it's written in human language and communication styles, their understanding is limited to foundational principles that can lead them to salvation. The Holy Spirit's role for the believer is to guide them into deeper, more advanced knowledge—the revelational knowledge about God and the mysteries of the Gospel. An unbeliever is just one step away from receiving the Holy Spirit's guidance: believing in Christ Jesus.

Eighth, we must avoid certain common pitfalls to correctly understand the Bible. By pitfalls, we mean distractions or common practices that can lead us away from grasping God's true intent in His written Word. One such pitfall is approaching the Bible with preconceived ideas based on traditional teachings, causing us to ignore what we read in favor of those traditions. A clear example is questioning why a good person would go to the lake of fire just because they didn't believe in Christ Jesus, as stated in the Bible.

We must also avoid reading Scripture with preconceived opinions or relying solely on the teachings of authorities or handed-down doctrines. It's important to check traditional beliefs and conventional ideas while reading the Bible so we don't let them override what the Word says. Similarly, we should not let our worldview precede what the Bible teaches. Relying too heavily on the opinion of a well-known pastor or authority figure without proof is another trap to avoid.

It's crucial to let go of a "know-it-all" attitude and remain open to learning, especially when someone presents a sound argument fully backed by Scripture. Another common mistake is placing too much emphasis on the original languages of the Bible, such as digging into Greek and Hebrew words and changing their English translations. Doing this suggests that the English Bible we read from is untrustworthy and that we doubt God's promise to preserve His Word. If God promised to preserve His Word, He must have done so. The versions of the Bible that have endured through the ages are likely His preserved Word. Great care and guidance from the Holy Spirit went into selecting the words used in translation, so there is no need to change them—it would be like trying to correct God. Consistently applying the outlined approach above in our Bible studies will open the door to understanding the messages God has preserved for us in the Bible.

Once you begin to see Jesus Christ as the central theme of the entire Bible, it may be a sign of scriptural clarity. Jesus himself mentioned this in John 5:39. He said:

"Search the scriptures; for in them ye think ye have eternal life: and they are they which testify of me."

This indicates that searching the Scriptures is meant to lead to eternal life, but ultimately, Jesus is the end of that search. This should be easy to understand if we realize that Jesus is the giver of eternal life. Therefore, when you find Jesus in the Scriptures, He will grant you eternal life. John echoes this idea in John 20:31:

"But these (the Bible) *are written, that ye might believe that Jesus is the Christ, the Son of God; and that believing ye might have life* (eternal life) *through his name."*

12

FINAL WORDS

What is it all about? Writing a book of this kind transcends simple enthusiasm or the enjoyment of arranging words on a page. It is established as a duty to restore clarity to those who engage with the Bible, enabling them to properly understand the message that God has imparted within the scriptures. Understanding scripture over the years has been like the story of the three blind men who went to view an elephant, each touching different parts of an elephant. The one who felt the ear had a different view from the one who touched the trunk, and another who touched the legs. Each had his distinct view. However, an elephant has one definite shape, requiring a clear vision. Herein lies an undeniable need to reach out to believers who have been lost in the shadows of false teachings, trapped in the torment that ignorance breeds. Therefore, the need to craft this work is about shedding light on the darkness that blinds to rescue those suffocating under the weight of distorted doctrines and lost vision.

How about the sermons you consume and their opposing doctrinal stances? One listening to certain preachers who, with great fervor and Bibles in hand, passionately argue the numerous justifications for tithing, for instance, is simultaneously confronted by other preachers presenting a compelling case against tithing for Christians, drawing their reasoning from the very same scriptures that the former preachers uphold. You are left dangling in confusion without knowing whose side to be on. But who is telling the truth? Then your option would be to ask the question, what does the bible say about this? This is why this book is written. To provide tools in the hands of those believers who dare to ask what the mind of God is amidst these controversies surrounding parading God's men.

The poison of false doctrines spreads far beyond the victim, it infects families, corrodes friendships, and eats away at communities. Entire nations can crumble under its weight, their people bound by spiritual chains, their minds tormented by beliefs that twist the truth. We've seen this darkness rise recently, with African countries standing as haunting examples of how deeply these deceptions can infiltrate and destroy.

They prey on the African man's deep reverence and tender-heartedness to God, selling him a twisted, other gospel that has no roots in scripture. This false gospel, crafted with sinister precision, is designed to manipulate and enrich a select few, leaving the masses in spiritual and financial ruin. The impoverished, blind to the truth, embrace their suffering, passionately defending the leaders who keep them shackled in deception. How could they know? How could they see through the manipulation and ignorance of the ones they trust when their faith has been weaponized against them? How can one recognize the wrong without knowing the right? But how could they ever see the right when they don't even read the Book—the Bible—the only true source and keeper of the truth? This is exactly what Jesus spoke of in Matthew 22:29. How can they turn to the Bible when convinced it's too difficult to understand? This is the tragedy, and it's why this book exists—to help you unlock the treasure within that seemingly impenetrable shell, to awaken your mind and stir your soul to seek the way out of the darkness of error.

The West is not immune to the relentless assault on Christianity and the Bible, nor to the crisis brewing within Christendom. Church attendance interest has been steadily declining across cultures in the West, and at the heart of this decay lies the spread of misinformation and distortion of Scripture. Those responsible are either blind to the truth or deliberately manipulating it for personal gain or status. Recently, Christian congregations have become more like mere social gatherings and places of pleasure, entertainment, and networking. The scripture is relegated while philosophy, works of literature, and poetry are elevated, leading to weak and psychical congregations that lack the demonstration of the power of the spirit of God. The Christian faith in various lesser-discussed regions of the world is not immune to these recent crises, among numerous others.

Not forgetting about the vast majority of us universally, who are strategically dislodged from accessing the need for personal study of the Word, and whose only hope is in the authenticity of their denomination rather than the salvation our Lord gives. We are not talking about the rest of the unsaved, whom the Lord will reach through the saved. It is imperative, therefore, that we learn how to read and understand Scripture, to be clear on what is required of us, and function perfectly in our predestined role.

Amidst all this darkness, there is one beautiful message I must deliver to you, a message of hope. The true Gospel of Christ shall continue to spread. The same God who inspired and preserved His Word will ensure its propagation according to His will. But we must know that God works through human vessels. If you choose to be one, you could become a battle axe in His hands, to wage war against the darkness that seeks to obscure the truth. That's why this book is written—to equip you with the tools necessary to discern God's mind in the Bible, to arm you with the truth. I sincerely desire this book to empower you to know the truth and stand for the truth.

Index

A

Abraham, 93, 106, 112, 115

Acts, 5, 9, 16, 25, 32, 48, 69, 93, 99, 109, 110, 127, 130, 131, 163

Agone, 28

American Standard Version (ASV), 22

Amos, 5

Animal Hides, 6

Anthropomorphism, 54

Apostle, 8, 11, 87, 125

Apostle's Application, 111

Aramaic, 14, 154

Argumentum, 150

Astrology, 50

Atonement, 107

B

Babylonian, 9, 93

Baptism, 133

Beseech, 28

Bronze Serpent, 116

C

Cardiac, 51

Christendom, 59, 60, 170

Christians' Faith, 4

Christ's Deity, 30

Chronicles, 5, 93, 103

Clean Heart, 51

Colossians, 5, 96, 119, 141, 159

Comely, 28

Congregations, 67, 171

Corinth, 9

Corinthians, 5, 8, 58, 59, 60, 61, 66, 101, 116, 124, 125, 126, 132, 143, 160

Covenant, 89, 104, 106

A practical guide to scriptural clarity

Crucifixion, 8, 98

Cuneiform Script, 6

D

Daniel, 5, 9, 103

Dearth, 28

Decipher, 61

Deuteronomy, 5, 78, 101, 117, 118, 119

Diermēneusen, 87

Divorce, 75

Doctrine, 4, 36, 46, 61, 64, 66, 97, 99, 111, 127, 130, 132, 134, 160

E

Ecclesiastes, 5, 71, 103

Echo, 35, 95

English Standard Version (ESV), 15, 20

Ephesians, 5, 104, 109, 119, 125

Epistles Of Paul, 114, 131, 132

Esther, 5, 9, 103

Ethiopian Eunuch, 69

Ethiopian Orthodox Church, 5

Evangelical Churches, 24

Exodus, 5, 6, 93, 94, 95, 101, 107, 116

Extol, 28

Ezekiel, 3, 5, 9

Ezra, 5, 93, 103

F

Flashcards, 37

G

Galatians, 5, 97, 106, 114, 115

Galileo Galilei, 49

Garden Of Eden, 95

Genesis, 5, 26, 43, 54, 64, 67, 92, 95, 101, 106, 109, 115, 130, 131

Global Positioning System (GPS), 70

God Of Israel, 2

Goodspeed, 28

Gospel, 80, 91, 100, 169

Grace Era, 94, 96, 107, 112, 114, 116

Greek, 14, 27, 87, 105, 154, 156, 166

H

Habakkuk, 3, 5, 80

Haggai, 5

Hebrews, 5, 66, 88, 96, 101, 104, 107, 109, 110, 112, 117, 126, 150

Holy Ghost, 25, 27, 153

'Holy Spirit, 25, 27

H

Hosea, 5, 54

I

Indecent Dressings, 82

Isaiah, 3, 5, 67, 68, 85, 90, 92

Israel, Iii, 7, 9, 89, 93, 118

J

James, Iii, 5, 15, 16, 18, 20, 21, 22, 25, 26, 27, 30, 144, 153, 155, 157

Jehovah, 86

Jeremiah, 2, 5, 89

Jewish, 9, 11

Job, 5, 103

Joel, 5, 103

John, 5, 7, 8, 10, 15, 16, 23, 29, 35, 41, 48, 53, 54, 55, 57, 62, 66, 76, 93, 96, 98, 109, 117, 120, 122, 126, 127, 130, 131, 134, 142, 148, 150, 161, 164, 167

Jonah, 3, 5

Joshua, 5, 49, 93, 137, 138, 141

Jude, 5, 163

Judges, 5, 93, 94

Juggling, 43

K

Ketuvim, 100, 103

Kindergartens, 124

A practical guide to scriptural clarity

King James Version (KJV), 15, 18, 157

Kings, 5, 93

L

Lamentations, 5, 66, 103

Layman's Moon, 49

Leviticus, 5, 101, 107

Licensure Exams, 37

Lucifer, 67

Luke, 5, 7, 9, 32, 38, 87, 90, 92, 96, 99, 130, 131

M

Malachi, 5, 7, 75, 95, 130, 131

Man's Redemption, 111

Mark, 5, 23, 96, 130, 131

Matthew, 5, 9, 13, 15, 32, 33, 40, 41, 52, 54, 76, 93, 95, 98, 101, 130, 131, 164, 170

Melchizedek's Priesthood, 113

Metaphor, 52, 53, 54, 159

Micah, 3, 5

Millennial Reign Era, 94

Miracles, 76

Mosaic Law, 95, 105

Moses, 6, 7, 94, 116

Mount Sinai, 95

N

Nehemiah, 5, 93, 103

New American Standard Bible (NASB), 20

New International Version (NIV), 15, 20, 23

New King James Version (NKJV), 16, 20, 25, 30, 157

New Living Translation (NLT), 20

Nicodemus, 29, 126

O

Obadiah, 5

Old Covenant, 7, 8, 100, 132

Old Testament, 7, 8, 95, 130, 132

P

Paradox, 54

Patriarchal Period, 93, 94

Patriarchs, 93, 113

Pauline Epistles, 111

Pentateuch, 6, 101

Pentecost, 8, 103, 163

Pentecostal Churches, 24

Peter, 3, 5, 9, 61, 81, 116, 134

Philemon, 5, 109, 110, 111

Philippians, 5, 24, 153

Pre-Law Era, 94, 107, 112, 115

Protestants, 5

Proverbs, 5, 66, 68, 69, 103, 119, 130, 132, 164

Psalms, 5, 103, 130, 132, 150, 164

R

Revelational Knowledge, 77, 126

Romans, 5, 48, 58, 60, 61, 71, 80, 83, 90, 95, 97, 104, 109, 111, 112, 114, 115, 119, 128, 132, 140, 142

Rome, 9

Ruth, 5, 103

S

Samuel, 5, 93

Satan, 67, 68, 150

Sayest, 28

Scriptures, 3, 7, 15, 35, 37, 78, 109, 113, 121, 123, 127, 142, 167, 168, 169

Sexual Immorality, 74

Sexual Urges, 74

Song of Solomon, 5, 103

Symbolic Representation, 33

Synecdoche, 55

T

Taketh, 25, 28, 117

Tantamount, 101

Textus Receptus, 18, 27, 155

The Bible, Vii, 1, 4, 10, 13, 33, 50, 54, 78, 88, 92, 123, 136, 162

Thessalonians, 5, 96

Timothy, 1, 4, 5, 35, 36, 37, 70, 87, 88, 94, 105, 108, 113, 154, 162

Titus, 5, 127

Tomounta, 87

Torah, 11, 100, 102

Tribulation era, 96

U

United Kingdom, 94

V

Verecundiam, 150

W

Wardrobe, 82

Z

Zechariah, 5

Zephaniah, 5

ABOUT THE AUTHOR

Dr. Chika I. Egeruo is a songwriter, a preacher, and a teacher of the Gospel. He is the president and founder of Stitch Music Int'l. He has an unwavering commitment to sharing the gospel of Jesus Christ. Aside from the ministry, this author maintains a day job in healthcare. He aims to inspire and enlighten readers with insights and genuine love for the gospel.

www.ingramcontent.com/pod-product-compliance
Lightning Source LLC
LaVergne TN
LVHW012107070526
838202LV00056B/5656